CU00722908

God Riddance

Contents

PREFACE   2
GOD RIDDANCE; AN INTRODUCTION   4
HUMANISM; WHAT IS IT AND DO WE NEED IT?   6
GOD, THE AFTERLIFE AND MORALITY   17
HATE CRIME AND PUBLIC ORDER (SCOTLAND) ACT 2022   23
NATIONALISM AND THE CALL FOR INDEPENDENCE: THE UK AND SCOTLAND   36
THE SOCIAL CONTRACT   49
ANIMAL WELFARE (ANIMAL SENTIENCE, CRUELTY, LEGAL PROTECTION AND RIGHTS.)   63
CLIMATE CHANGE AND GLOBAL WARMING   74
STOICISM   93
MIND AND BODY; DETERMINISM AND FREE WILL   98
JUST WAR, OR JUST WAR?   105
GOD RIDDANCE; A CONCLUSION   123
INDEX   125

Humanist Society of Scotland [HSS] is a non-prophet organisation without any invisible means of support. This booklet is produced with a view to proceeds going towards HSS and its work in Scotland.

Author; Dr Martin MacEwen
Publisher: Vektor Publishing
Printer: Imprint Digital
ISBN: 978-1-917010-45-0

Preface

As Chief Executive of Humanist Society Scotland, I am honoured to be asked to introduce Dr Martin MacEwen's enlightening book, "God Riddance." This work aligns with our mission to embed humanist values in Scottish society, offering a concise yet profound exploration of a humanist's perspective on pressing contemporary issues. The Humanist Society Scotland is a vibrant charity committed to fostering a caring, compassionate, and rational Scotland. Our society advocates for a secular democracy where human rights, autonomy, and dignity are upheld for all. We achieve this through a diverse range of activities, including educational outreach, high-quality ceremonies, and impactful campaigns on issues such as secular education, reproductive rights, and end-of-life care.

In recent years, we have celebrated significant milestones. Over 18,000 members strong, our community has supported thousands of humanist ceremonies, ensuring meaningful and personalised celebrations for life's key events. Our campaigns have seen substantial successes, including scrapping the Scottish blasphemy law, legal recognition of same-sex marriage, the removal of religious voting rights from a number local education committees and advocacy for safe access zones for abortion services. These achievements underscore our dedication to creating a society that respects and reflects its non-religious population.

However, the journey is far from over. Despite a majority of Scots identifying as non-religious, religious privilege persists in various facets of public life, from media representation to legislative processes. This enduring influence challenges the principle of equality and often sidelines secular voices. Dr. MacEwen's book addresses this imbalance by presenting a reasoned argument for a society where morality and meaning are derived from human connections and community support rather than religious dogma.

"God Riddance" serves as a vital resource, presenting humanism not as an abstract philosophy but as a practical, ethical approach to life. It tackles topics ranging from nationalism and social contracts to animal welfare and stoicism, each chapter inviting readers to consider how humanist values can shape a more just and rational society.

The challenges facing humanists in contemporary Scotland are manifold. Our continued efforts to promote secularism in education, protect individual rights, and advocate for rational policies are crucial in the face of persistent religious influence. By fostering dialogue, supporting evidence-based policies, and providing inclusive platforms for non-religious voices, we can challenge the role religion plays in Scottish public life. There is a growing force of simplistic populism entering our political and public life, both at home and overseas that threatens the very principles of democracy that humanists hold so dear, and that we know is the cornerstone to freedom, liberty and equality.

Looking forward, our strategic plan for 2024-2027 outlines ambitious goals. We aim to nurture and expand our community, enhance our ceremonies, and amplify our advocacy on critical public policy issues. By building bridges with allied groups and ensuring our digital presence is strong and accessible, we strive to make humanist values a cornerstone of Scottish society.

Dr. MacEwen's "God Riddance" is a timely contribution to this ongoing dialogue. It not only educates but also inspires action towards a fairer, more inclusive Scotland. As we continue our work, we remain grateful for the unwavering support of our members, volunteers, and partners. Together, we can champion a Scotland where secularism, compassion, and reason prevail.

Fraser Sutherland
Chief Executive

Humanist Society Scotland
Registered Address: Suite 25, 4 Lochside Way, Edinburgh Park, EH12 9DT
Humanist Society Scotland is a registered Scottish charity (SC 026570) and a Scottish Company limited by guarantee, registered under Company Number 413697.

God Riddance; an Introduction

The purpose of this short book is to introduce readers to some of the thoughts and approaches adopted by Humanists towards a selection of issues facing us today. Over 50% of the Scottish population claim to have no religion and no doubt a large percentage of that sector have no belief in a god or gods. Despite that, whether through 'Thought for the Day', Sunday God Slots or similar media outputs, the concept of monotheism and morality dependent on it are promoted. The Humanist would not want to deny such outlets nor the potential benefits which may well stem from such beliefs but would argue that a like opportunity to state the godless case should be afforded, particularly on state-funded media. That being denied gives credence to a view that without god, morality is bereft of guidance and direction and life has no meaning.

There is a plethora of books on Humanism (as exemplified by the list at the end) and it may be asked why add another, even if it is of an introductory and select nature. Indeed, that is the primary reason. Many of us lead busy and absorbing lives and feel disinclined to devote much time to what may appear vague, philosophical and distant to our immediate concerns. This book in its brevity and its selection of some topical and some apparently more obscure issues is an attempt to overcome such disinclination and to provide the reader with a short but thought-provoking read relevant to his or her interests.

It is the contention of humanists that morality is derived from our social interactions and our belief that a wholesome, fulfilling and meaningful life is more likely to arise from our interdependence, our innate sense of community and the need for mutual support, rather than the fear of god induced retribution of punishment for wrongdoing, or the promise of a heavenly afterlife for following the mantra of particular scriptures. After the Egyptians, it has been argued, organised religion is the world's largest pyramid scheme. But to the humanist, it is not remarkable that many who live without god, such as Buddhists or Stoics, enjoy such meaningful and fulfilling lives and are admired for this. The selection of topics while not exactly arbitrary, is not of necessity all of primary importance. Certainly, the chapters on Humanism, on Hate Crime, on Animal Welfare, on Just War, on Nationalism and Independence are of contemporary concern but the issues in the chapters on Social Contract, on life after death, Mind and Matter and Determinism may appear more ephemeral. It is also true that major concerns including famine, poverty and equality are not addressed here, but that may be for another day?

Meanwhile, let me acknowledge the debt to Wikipedia, Encyclopaedia Britannica Online and Philosophy Now, in particular, which have provided a wealth of factual background and material for rational discussion on the various topics addressed.

The idea for this booklet stemmed from a local Edinburgh Humanist discussion group whose monthly meetings addressed many of the topics for discussion here. The idea had been for the group members, or as many as felt inclined, to contribute to this publication. While that objective proved illusive, for multifarious reasons, I would like to record my thanks to the group, as listed below;

Les Reid, Richard and Jackie Grant, David Wilson and Theresa Wilson, Alex Simpson, Neil Macdonald, Anne Murray and Martin Torzewski.

Thanks, also, to Fraser Sutherland, as CEO of HSS a key player in the Humanist cause, and my daughter Zoe MacEwen Trokic who, unstintingly, kept the machinery working, as well as my other daughter Fiona Morgan, her husband Peter Morgan and Jessica, my wife, all of whose helpful advice was largely ignored until its wisdom was unavoidable.

May I also extend my thanks to Vektor Publishing for their help on the text and Index in particular.

Happy reading.

Martin

1. Debating Humanism, Dolan Cummings, ed., Societas, 2006
2. On Humanism, Richard Norman, Routledge, 2004
3. Humanism, an Introduction, Jim Herrick, Prometheus Books, 2003
4. The Quotable Atheist, Jack Huberman, Nation Books, 2007
5. Humanist Anthology, Margaret Knight, ed, Rationalist Press Association, 1961
6. Enlightenment Now, Steven Pinker, Penguin Books, 2018
7. The Little Book of Humanism, Andrew Copson and Alice Robert, Piatkus, 2020
8. The Good Book; A Secular Bible, A C Grayling, Bloomsbury, 2011
9. The Moral Landscape, Sam Harris, Transworld Publishing, 2010

Humanism; What is it and do we need it?

Brief history of the origins of Humanism

Prominent Greek and later Roman Scholars and philosophers, namely Socrates, Plato and Aristotle and the Stoic adherents were instrumental in setting the foundations of humanism. While a belief in a God or Gods often permeated their teachings, there was also an appeal to rational inquiry and a willingness to challenge accepted norms. The creation of the Senate and the power of the Consuls as well as the writings of Cicero (106-43 BC) alluded to the concept of democracy and the idea of power-sharing as well as the rule of law, however inchoate in the Roman system of governance.

The teachings and doctrine adopted and promoted by both St. Augustine in the 4th century and Thomas Aquinas in the 13 century reflected much of the ideology underpinning Humanism if not the belief, necessarily, in monotheism; the golden rule- do as you would be done by-, respect for human life and learning as a necessary part of development, particularly after the invention of the printing press, were common aspirations.

Similar beliefs could be found in Confucianism, Islam, Hinduism and particularly Buddhism where a belief in God or Gods was optional. During the Renaissance Petrarch (1304-1374) was important in the rediscovery of Cicero and his 'Pro Archia'; here he outlined 4 major disciplines forming the basis of humanism, namely, rhetoric, moral philosophy, poetry and grammar. This influenced education in schools in Italy particularly. Teachings and the press spread humanism to northern Europe and by the end of the 15th century, Erasmus had become the leading Humanist Scholar. In his De Libero Animo (On Free Will) he challenged Luther's assertion that humans are corrupt sinners whose fate is predestined. Education and prayer were seen as important vehicles in reforming the Roman Catholic church.

In the era of the Enlightenment, Spinoza (1632-1677) argued that God was not the creator of the world, but the world was part of God, a form of pantheism conflicting with both Jewish and Christian teaching. What humanists believed and what shaped their ethics and morality at that time may have differed from one group to another, but it was Hume who argued that humanism was strongly linked to rationality, personal experience and scientific discovery. Kant (1724-1804), believed in transcendental realism; this distinguished what we can experience- the natural observable world- and the 'super-sensible' which is beyond experience, such as God and the soul. However, the motivating idea was to remove intellectual activity away from the shackles of religion and to infuse human life with knowledge rather than the fear of God or the assurance of his mercy.

This process continued throughout the 19th and 20th centuries, the age of scientific rationalism witnessing Darwinism, Freudism, quantum mechanics and significant advances in medicine. The shift, it has been argued, was from intellectual hierarchies to pluralism, from certainty to inquiry. Similarly, artistic realism imbued with guilt such as Dostoevsky (1821-1881) and Zola (1840-1902), gave way to documentary realism by Dreiser (1871-1945) and Wells (1866-1946). Humanism then developed an avowedly anti-religious stance.

Contemporary interests

Corliss Lamont (1902-1995) in his 'The Philosophy of Humanism' (1949, revised 1997) was important in setting out largely accepted beliefs and values of contemporary humanist philosophy. In his book 'The Affirmative Ethics of Humanism' he suggested: -

The greatest difference between the Humanist ethic and that of Christianity and the traditional religions is that it (Humanism) is entirely based on happiness in this one and only life and is not concerned with a realm of supernatural mortality and the glory of God.

Humanism denies the philosophical and psychological dualism of soul and body and contends that a human being is a oneness of mind, personality and physical organism. Christian insistence on the resurrection of the soul and on personal immortality has severed the nerve of effective action here and now, and has led to the neglect of present human welfare and happiness.

Margaret Knight (1903-1983) assembled a useful anthology of humanist writings from Confucius to David Attenborough. In her Introduction (1961) she stated that the term 'Humanist' had changed appreciably in the years from 1900, noting Wittgenstein's observation that the meaning of a word is the way in which it is used. Today the term implies that the Humanist sees no reason to believe in a supernatural God or in life after death. Virtue, she went on to say, is a matter of promoting human well-being and that the mainsprings of moral action are what Darwin termed as moral instincts- those altruistic, co-operative tendencies that are as much part of our innate biological make-up as tendencies towards aggression and cruelty.

As Pinker (2019) states, Humanist morality rests on the bedrock of reason and human interests; it is an inescapable feature of the human condition that we are all better off if we help each other and refrain from hurting each other. As a consequence, many contemporary philosophers including Peter Singer, Peter Railton, Richard Boyd, Davis Brink and Peter Parfit are moral realists arguing that moral statements are inherently true or false in contradistinction to the relativists who may be supported by much religious doctrine.

Humanism, A.C. Grayling asserts (2009), denoted a family of views premised on the commitment to the idea that ethics and social policy must be based on our best understanding of human nature and the human condition. It is a starting point, not a finished body of doctrine. Referring to Cicero, 'there is nothing so like anything else as we are to one another'. The foundation of this bond should consist of kindness, generosity, goodness and justice.

The Humanist Manifestos

Steven Pinker refers to the 1933 Humanist Manifesto being one of a trilogy; the Humanist Manifesto 111 from 2003, in brief states: -

Humans are an integral part of nature, the result of unguided evolutionary change.
Ethical values are derived from human needs and interests as tested by experience.
Life's fulfilment emerges from individual participation in the service of humane ideals.
Humans are social in nature and find meaning in relationships. Humanists strive towards a world of mutual care and concern.
Working to benefit society maximises individual happiness.

Many Humanist Associations were established both between the World Wars, and after, where such values were promoted and even religious groups including Lutherans, Quakers, Unitarians and liberal branches of Episcopalians and Judaism adopted Humanist values, frequently soft-pedalling their legacies of belief in the supernatural and even ecclesiastical authority in favour of reason and human flourishing.

Amsterdam Declaration 1952, 2002 and Glasgow 2022

There are a number of definitions of contemporary Humanism but perhaps one of the most authoritative is that provided by the Amsterdam Declaration of 1952 as amended in 2002 and by the 2022 World Humanism Conference in Glasgow. This amended declaration has much in common with the principles in the Manifestos outlined above.

This, in summary, proclaims that Humanist beliefs and values have a history around the world and are a culmination of long traditions of reasoning about meaning and ethics and are interwoven with the rise of modern science. There are four key points in the revised declaration.

Firstly, humanists strive to be ethical; they accept that morality is inherent in the human condition, motivated by helping and not harming. Recognising the worth and dignity of the individual, all have a right to freedom and development so far as compatible with like rights in others; to these ends, they support peace, democracy, the rule of law and universal legal human rights. All forms of racism and prejudice and injustices that so arise are rejected. They hold that personal liberty must be combined with social responsibility and a duty of care to all humans and future generations and to all sentient beings. Being part of nature humanists have a responsibility on our impact on the rest of the world.

Secondly, humanists strive to be rational; solutions to the world's problems lie in human reason and action; while science may provide the means, human values must define the ends to be sought. Science and technology must be used to enhance human well-being and not used destructively.

Thirdly, Humanists strive for fulfilment in their lives; all sources of joy and fulfilment that inflict no harm to others are valued. Personal development through the cultivation of creative and ethical living is a lifelong undertaking. Artistic creativity and imagination are treasured and the transformative power of literature, music and the visual and performing arts is recognised, as is the beauty of the natural world and its ability to bring wonder, awe and tranquillity. Individual and communal activity is encouraged as is the comradeship and sense of achievement it offers. The quest for knowledge is esteemed with the humility, wisdom and insight it bestows.

Fourthly, humanism contends that it meets the widespread demand for a source of meaning and purpose as an alternative to dogmatic religion, authoritarian nationalism, tribal sectarianism and selfish nihilism. Humanists accept that knowledge of the world and humankind can only be achieved through a continuing process of observation, learning and rethinking. Accordingly, it seeks not to avoid scrutiny nor to impose its view on all humanity; but rather it seeks to co-operate with people of different beliefs who share its values to build a better world. Humanity, it is argued, has the potential to solve problems through free inquiry, science, sympathy, and imagination in the furtherance of peace and human flourishing and it asks those who share these convictions to join humanists in this endeavour.

Humanist Morality

The humanist view moved from a universal human narrative underlying Kantian ethics to greater flexibility in a changing attitude to moral behaviour influenced by advances in science as well as greater social tolerance to the previous norms. This has led to support for egalitarianism, civil rights, personal responsibility, religious toleration and multiculturalism. Morality, it has been argued, may not be hardwired to humans within their evolution but may be derived from selfish self-interest. A contrary view, as articulated by John Shook, Brian Ellis, and Andrew Copson amongst others suggests that moral naturalism relates to our genetic makeup and social interdependence implying that human traits are inclined to human welfare. Leaning on Hume's naturalism and empathy, Aristotle's theory of virtue, based on the Stoic's concept of eudaimonia [happiness, in the sense of having a good, desirable and fulfilling life], and Kant's idealism, morality involves individual integrity, a social awareness and concern and an aim not only for personal fulfilment but also for human welfare.

Humanism and The Meaning of Life

It may be argued that Camus and his allusion to the Myth of Sisyphus points to personal agency and self-determination which lies at the centre of humanism. The purpose of living has to be in marrying individual growth [whether intellectual, artistic, physical attainment or musical or creative development] with a meaningful contribution to social improvement and development.

Politics and Secularism

While humanists advocate tolerance towards all religious faiths, they consider the impact of religious faith on politics including educational curricula and representation to elected bodies to be detrimental to the non-partisan needs of society generally and liberal democracy in particular; this is best served by secular independence from the dominance of one faith or another and the influence of superstition and irrational hypothesis.

Criticism

Critics of Humanism variously refer to:-

1. the implications of a western Western bias (Asad, 2020) ignoring like traditions from India and China, for example.
2. An unquestioning acceptance of the Human Rights agenda and the promotion of individual expression at the expense of social concerns.
3. Humanism is said to be anthropocentric; it either ignores man as being in and of nature or casts man as the new god, mastering the world and controlling all.
4. It is also accused of being Utopian and promoting an unattainable influence of mankind on world improvement [Reference, for example, John Gray (2014), Yuval Harari (2016).
5. Are humanist values a tool of Western dominance? we are asked; a sort of neo-colonialism leading to the oppression of monotheists. Because of its origins, it may fail to adequately represent women, black activists, and gay and lesbian advocates (Childers and Hentzi, 1995).
6. Further criticism, mainly from evangelical Christians is that Humanism destroys traditional family life and moral values. This has been denounced by some as a malicious campaign by religious fanatics, the so-called Moral Majority.
7. Others suggest it is materialistic in that humans are seen as physical systems in a scientific world, and this denies the spiritual needs of man.
8. Another criticism is that the meaning of the term is so vague that it appears a semantic cloud of meanings and implications, non-attached to any particular theory or practitioner (Sarah Bakewell, 2023). Andrew Copson (2015) acknowledges that the existence of two types of Humanism, secular and religious, tends to muddy the waters.

9. Perhaps humanism is merely utilitarianism in another form.
10. Nietzsche argued that Humanism harboured a number of illusions, especially the nature of truth. In his view, truth is an anthropomorphic illusion; humanism is meaningless, replacing theism and science and reason simply usurps one religion with another (Davies, 1997).

Resolution

1. While it is true that the dominant origins of Humanism are derived from Greek and Roman pre-Christian philosophy, there are significant similarities with Buddhism, Hindu and Chinese and general Confucian approaches and values. Humanist thought in Asia has a long, distinguished history, traceable to hundreds of years BCE. This encompasses humanistic elements in the philosophies of Confucianism and Buddhism, as well as explicitly agnostic or atheist schools of thought, like the Lokayata and Ajñana of India. Nicholas F. Gier has described Buddhism and Confucianism as 'humanistic in the sense that neither view requires divine aid for attaining liberation or achieving the good life'. Further, in the path towards enlightenment, Buddha embraced scepticism. Scepticism, from the Greek term skeptikoi, is adopting an inquiring state of mind, challenging the status quo or dogmatic establishments and concepts, and thus advancing critical thinking. Buddha utilised such a mindset to reject beliefs imposed by authoritative figures, scriptures, hearsay, or legends, thus attaining liberation and self-actualisation, with the freedom to experience life, determine what is good or bad, what is conducive to self-growth, and how our actions affect others (see also Robert Wright, 2018).

   African humanism is primarily and philosophically realised in ubuntu: a Bantu word meaning 'humanity' or 'humanness.' Often explained by the phrase 'I am because we are'; ubuntu is community-based thinking, rooted in the idea that our humanity is developed through community and connection with others. As Clive Aruede (2021) of the Association of Black Humanists puts it: Ubuntu means 'I am, because you are'. Ubuntu is part of the Zulu phrase 'Umuntu ngumuntu ngabantu', meaning that we are human only through the humanity of others.

2. It in its support for democratic rule-based government and Human Rights, it is conceded that it eschews autocratic and dogmatic leadership as evidenced in certain Marxist, Muslim and Born Again Christian

movements such as 'Make America Great Again'; if that is a weakness, most humanists would see this as a strength.

3. Again, Humanists would accept that it is anthropocentric in the sense that while the human being may not be the only sentient animal, it is the one best placed to effect beneficial change while recognising that it is part of nature and there are clearly limits to what is achievable. It would also admit to being anthropocentric in the sense that it believes men/women have a critical role in promoting not only human well-being but also in acknowledging that there is an interdependence with the natural world, animals, plants and the bio-system; humans have a moral duty to protect the environment and to counter the forces that extinguish species, including the ravages of climate change.

4. In such recognition, the humanist does not claim to aspire to any Utopian vision, rather a pragmatic and realistic view while recognising that it is part of nature which may assist improvements and provide a sense of individual and group fulfilment. Harari (2016) offers no evidence to support his assertion of the humanist aspiration to cosmic control but his claim that their dominant values attach to liberal individualism is a more coherent charge. Moreover, his assertion that democratic values may be used by technical and other influences to promote individual gain at the expense of communal concerns, perhaps illustrated by the dangers of global warming, provides a clear warning that democratic and human values of social welfare may be threatened by developing and insidious influences.

5. Humanists argue that individual fulfilment has to be balanced with human well-being and improvement. It is doubtful whether these are peculiarly Western values or whether they comprised a tool of colonial oppression. In the espousal of tolerance and inclusion, the argument that minorities are sidelined by Humanism is challenged by the various campaigns humanist associations have initiated and supported as well as the number of African and Asian Humanist Associations. While the Declaration of Amsterdam 2022 expresses its opposition to authoritarian nationalism and tribal sectarianism, in its support for peace and democracy it, implicitly, supports freedom from colonial rule and the right of democratically elected states to determine their future subject to the retention of values relating to the promotion of both individual and social human rights. It is said the Universal Declaration of Human Rights is a humanist manifesto (Pinker 2018). In 1948 it was passed without

opposition by the UN General Assembly. Contrary to the accusation that human rights are a parochial Western creed, the Declaration was supported by India, China, Thailand, Ethiopia, and seven Muslim countries. The Soviet bloc, Saudi Arabia and apartheid South Africa abstained while the States, concerned about domestic racial discrimination and segregation, and Britain concerned about its treatment of its colonies both had to be persuaded to sign.

6. The destruction of family life and traditional values is clearly a vague charge but there is little if any evidence to support this or like assertions. The basis for this accusation appears to be that moral rectitude is anathema to those who reject the belief in a god and a life after death. But the moral tenets of humanism have much in common with those of the major religions, except that such doctrines are unchallengeable, and god given. Moreover, the attitudes and prejudices of Mary Whitehouse and the National Festival of Light and their followers in the UK and the Moral Majority in the US, based on evangelical certainties, both seek to police and condemn attitudes and activities which challenge Christian mores and norms.

7. That Humanism is materialistic and denies the spiritual element of human existence is questionable. Certainly, it acknowledges the important place of science in determining who and where we are, but it also acknowledges the importance of the humanities, the word from which it is derived, in promoting meaning and well-being. Humanists counter the argument, that without religion and 'spiritual beliefs', ethics and morality are bereft, with the contention that religion and the belief in an afterlife threaten any challenge to their dogma with punishment in this life and with reward on death; this faith in fairies, the humanist argues, denies individual responsibility in the pursuit of a moral way of life. In its promotion of the transformative power of literature, music and the visual and performing arts as well as sport, Humanism recognises the limits of a purely materialistic approach to life.

8. Similarly, the accusation that Humanism is vague and shifts its position from time to time may be interpreted as a strength; it is not dogmatic and responds to scientific inquiry as well as changing social values.

9. With reference to the humanist's sympathy with utilitarianism, it is true that there is much in the analysis of Bentham and Mills regarding the decision-making for the general good with which humanists would agree but they would likely qualify any deontological or consequentialist

argument which leads to a conflict with developing ideas concerning humane treatment and human rights.

10. To accuse Humanism of replacing one form of religion for another is richly ironic. An accusation against secularism is that it fails to identify how a fulfilling life should be led. Now that Humanism articulates an approach which meets this criticism without dogma or false beliefs in an afterlife, it is then accused of creating another religion. To the extent that the Declaration of Amsterdam 2022 does articulate the Humanist understanding of how we all may live a meaningful individual and social existence, it may be classified as an approach but not a religious dogma.

Despite the specifics of the above critique, one of the most cogent and trenchant criticism of Humanism comes from an atheist, namely, John Gray (2014). In 'The Silence of the Animals' he states,
'For those who cannot bear to live without a belief, any faith is better than none. This is the appeal of fundamentalism which promises to banish the lack of meaning by an act of will. Hence also the god-building enthusiasm of humanists, who invite the arrival of a new deity, uglier than any that has ever before been worshipped, a divinised version of themselves...'Moreover in his diatribe 'Seven Types of Atheism' (2019) he refers to the assumption that Humanists believe not only in human improvement but also in their ability to influence such for the better. In respect of the former despite strong evidence that humankind is hell-bent on self-destruction and indeed destruction of the environment, there is some evidence to the contrary, as provided by Pinker (2017) who argues convincingly that the condition of human existence in respect of material well-being has advanced very significantly over the last ten decades. While he acknowledges the fact that such advances are not linear, in aggregate they are substantial. Although global warming with consequential drought, famine, floods, wildfires and tempests as well as wars and turmoil in the Ukraine, Israel, Yemen, Sudan and elsewhere may well challenge the assertion of progress, there is at least an aspiration that science, technology and human resource may effectively counteract the worst ravages of this. But it does remind us of the human propensity to self-destruct and the dangerous assumption that progress, in the sense of human well-being, is a given. Gray's assertion of Humanists creating a 'divinised' version of themselves is not only apocryphal but also blasphemy; he is fortunate that the blasphemy laws in Scotland have now been repealed and few today believe in the literal truth of the Old Testament!

It being acknowledged that progress is not a given and humankind does know how best to protect its own survival nor indeed the environment on which all life depends, the Humanist will believe that, even if such general progress is a myth or at least immediately thwarted or unattainable, there are benefits that remain in a positive attitude for both personal and communal well-being in striving to achieve whatever remains available. To deny that approach is to question, not the meaning of life, but whether the individual and communal approach to living will result in a fulfilling and productive livelihood.

References

Clive Aruede, Let's Talk about the African and Asian Origins of Humanism, Humanists International, 2021Corliss Lamont (1902-1995) 'The Philosophy of Humanism' [1949, revised 1997]
Margaret Knight, Humanist Anthology, Rational Press Association, 1961, revised 1975,
Steven Pinker, Enlightenment Now, Penguin Books, 2018
A C Grayling, Ideas that Matter, Phoenix Books, 2009
Yuval Noah Harari, Homo Deus, Vintage, 2016.
John Gray, Seven Types of Atheism, Penguin Random House, 2018
John Gray, The Silence of Animals, Penguin, 2014
Steven Pinker , Enlightenment Now, Penguin, 2019.
Sarah Bakewell, Humanly Possible, Penguin Press, 2023.
Andrew Copson, What is Humanism?, 2015.
Davies, Humanism, Psychology Press, 1997
Richard Norman, On Humanism, Routledge, 2004
Robert Wright, Why Buddhism is True, Simon and Schuster Paperbacks, 2017

God, the afterlife and morality

This chapter is going to explore the human need for a spiritual god and life after death and the morality of living a good life without either.

The life of man has moved from polytheism to monism. This has occurred over a period of not more than 300,000 years. During this time, many different forms of religion have been advocated. It is clearly not possible to believe in each of these forms. Accordingly, there seems little objective rational in accepting one form over another without proof of, or at least some convincing evidence to support, this contention. But, of course, religion is a matter of faith or belief, not proof, or even a convincing contention.

The life of the universe is estimated to be in the region of 13.75 billion years while the life of Earth is 4.5 billion years. As a consequence, and assuming that god gave rise to the universe, for the vast majority of time either god had ignored his creation, or his creatures had ignored or been oblivious of his existence. It is also difficult to comprehend why god has contemplated and sanctioned various types of devastation which have rid the earth of 90% of living creatures on occasion or settled on the creation of man so late on in the life of the universe, or even on our planet Earth.

God, it is argued, had some aim or purpose in the creation of life and designed its development. However, it is difficult to see any rational explanation relating to god's design or purpose, or indeed the purpose of the Cosmos (Tallis, 2024). Another explanation may be that god, having created the universe, went on a 13.749-billion-year sabbatical, leaving his creations and living beings, to fend for themselves. If that is the case, as Deist believe, there is no reason to worship an absent god nor to sing his or her praises. Similarly, there is no point in asking God for guidance in how life should be lived when he/she is not paying attention, nor has any interest in or influence on the events that follow.

As Douglas Adams observed 'isn't it enough to see that a garden is beautiful without having to believe that there are fairies at the bottom of it too? '

Most beliefs in a God assign him/her omnipresence, omniscience and eternity. The scriptures whether the Bible, the Koran or other holy texts have sought to explain the meaning of life and how it should be lived. Such books and writings are of contested if not dubious origin while, nonetheless, often offering sage advice. However, since the advent of the printing press, there has been a plethora of writings some of evident merit which offer guidance on how we should live. Such guidance has not of necessity depended on a presumption that it was god-given rather than man-made. Accordingly, the soundness of such advice does not depend on its origin but rather on its inherent value and wisdom.

One question demanding consideration is 'what is the ultimate cause of the universe?' If every action or occurrence has a preceding cause what was the originating cause, if not God? There are two more obvious answers to that. Firstly, if there is eternity, is there necessarily a first cause? Secondly, if there was a first cause on what basis should we invoke God as the originator as opposed to happen-stance. And when did God invent himself/herself?

Ockam's razor, looking for the simplest, most straightforward explanation, would eliminate God as the author on the basis that he/she has given no evidence to justify such a conclusion and many alternatives are more rational. Conversely, there is no absolute proof that God does not 'exist'. The same is true, however, for fairies at the bottom of the garden. Flew contends that it is for theists to prove the existence of the almighty rather than atheists to disprove it. Perhaps we should be like Woody Allen who, while admitting that he did not believe in an afterlife, said ' I'm bringing a change of underwear'.

Just as there is no objective reason to believe in a god, so there is no reason to believe in life after death. That being so, living in anticipation of an afterlife and, as a consequence, allowing our behaviour to be informed by either fear of or pleasure in what will follow death is misguided.

To base our moral judgments on this consideration is to deny the importance of our social interdependence on each other which, to a large extent, informs our sense of morality in a much more cogent and important way than apprehension of what will occur after we die.

Morality arises because humans are in essence social animals and cooperation, mutual tolerance and respect are necessary for individuals to live safe, peaceful, productive and fulfilling lives. Much of that wisdom comes from early Hindu, Buddhist and Confucianist philosophy, as well as the Greeks, in particular, Socrates [469-399 BC], Plato [428-348 BC] and Aristotle [384-322 BC]. But the Stoics, from the second century BC, as well as the Epicureans from the third century BC recognised this inter-dependence of the individual with society. It was their ideas that influenced Thomas Aquinas [1224-74 AD], in particular, in his articulation of the life that 'good' Christians should lead. In a similar vein of influence, the Enlightenment- from the Encyclopedists to Hume in the seventeenth century re-examined the Greek and Roman philosophers, without the Christian entrails, to conclude that a good life was not a necessary product of religious guidance.

Whether impelled by religious devotion or personal conviction, many will seek to lead a 'good life' in the sense of a life informed by a sense of morality embedded in fairness and justice. It may be that our personal circumstances, poverty, unemployment and lack of opportunity impose severe restrictions on life choices but there is still an expectation of fairness and justice. Sam Harris (2010) with reference to the concept of reciprocal altruism, admits that while there may remain much to explain about the biology of our moral impulses, such altruism, kin selection, and sexual selection provide a grounding for the development of common interests with others and why atomised self-interest is not the sole driving force of our interests and activities.

But what is a good life? Today, we are typically presented with three rival historical approaches. First, *consequentialism*, which says that moral life is a matter of determining which actions will produce the best results overall, and then performing those actions. Second, *deontology*, which involves discovering the rules or norms that guide good actions and obeying those rules. Third, *eudaimonism*. This term derives from the Greek word *eudaimonia*, which had the connotation of being 'blessed', but usually translates to 'happiness', flourishing, or fulfilment.

Consequentialism, as the name suggests, means that we judge actions by the results. This usually implies a utilitarian approach. The best result means the best for the largest number affected, and minimising disadvantage for the least. The gain against pain equation. Clearly this is not without difficulty as an approach. Should we indulge the prejudices of a majority irrespective of its moral worth? There are like dilemmas linked with a deontological approach. Doing the right thing irrespective of dire consequences. The bombing of Hiroshima and Nagasaki to end World War 11, may exemplify the dilemma. Theoretically the loss of life and horrendous impact thereafter was justifiable, in consequential terms, by the ending of the war with Japan and the resultant saving of thousands of lives as a result. Conversely was the bombing inherently morally wrong, just as any murder might be judged, irrespective of the consequences?

Eudaimonism argues that ethics is about figuring out how to flourish. But does this solve the above-described quandaries? Given the uncertainties which often ensue from the evaluation of potential gains against losses from adopting the consequentialist approach, many would prefer the ethics of the deontologist.

For Stoics, many aspects of life people might consider now as essential, such as wealth, health, reputation and a successful career, are considered externals.

"Whatever I possess, I shall neither hoard it greedily nor squander it needlessly", as Seneca observed [4 BCE-65 CE]. Thus, the wisdom of the Stoics is to use 'externals' wisely and not be overly attached to them. Our actions must be informed by our own conscience and not by the opinion of others although open and honest dialogue with others may rightly inform one's judgement. In contrast with indulgent consumerism which may reflect much of modern life, consumption of food and drink, for example, is to be tailored to our needs and not indulged to excess. Moreover, we are to treat others with care and consideration; the Stoic has no true foes, only humans who may be misguided in what they do or how they think. Stoics should be gentle and mild, we are told, and, as Seneca, observed, should be ready to forgive even before they are asked. Again, while it may be dangerous to idealise the Stoics, it is remarkable, given the contemporary fear of 'the other', particularly immigrants, that they advised while we should follow our inclinations to be kind and considerate to our family, friends and neighbours, there is no reason to treat others poorly just because they were fated to be born in a different place, look different or behave in unfamiliar ways. It is thus evident that the Stoics belief that Eudaimonia is the moral and fulfilling way to live and this attitude re-emerges in the philosophy of Emmanuel Kant who argued that the possession of 'good will' is an unconditional good. Today in 'Positive Psychology' we are asked to consider 6 dimensions of Eudaimonia, namely;

1. self-discovery;
2. perceived development of one's best potential;
3. a sense of purpose and meaning in life;
4. investment of significant effort in pursuit of excellence;
5. intense involvement in activities; and enjoyment of activities as personally expressive

Often it may be appropriate to apply the 'Golden Rule'; 'do unto others as you would be done by', This rule has its critics. Moral relativism implies that we should be cautious about applying our own unqualified perceptions and preconceptions. Should a white relatively well-off middle-class male assume his sense of justice and fairness, and attainment of well-being, would equate with the values held by a poor black working class, unemployed single parent in radically different circumstances? Despite that and other challenges to evaluation, the golden rule remains a helpful tool in assessing our thoughts and actions.

Across both religious and atheist divide, there appears to be a general agreement on what this moral and good life may entail. Firstly, it is not the pursuit of money, fame or power. As Spike Milligan observed, money may not buy you happiness, even if it may give you a luxury boat that anchors close by. Similarly, fame is ephemeral and will disappear when the element which underpins its rises then subsides from the lack of substance. Power, authority and influence may well be powerful aphrodisiacs, but they often are transitory and seldom give rise to a lasting sense of fulfilment. There is general agreement in philosophy, sociology and psychology that while a fruitful, full and rewarding life may be illusive, it depends on the fruits of altruism as much as personal achievement.

A view that Humanists would endorse and that James Hemming (1969) observed, 'The meaning of life is to live it as wholly as we can, as bravely as we can, here and now, sharing the experience with others, caring for others as we care for ourselves, and accepting our responsibility for leaving the world better than we found it.' Such an approach involving duties as well as rights may well be onerous. In a time of wars and natural disasters caused, or contributed to, by climate change from global warming, the fulsome or flourishing life need not require the individual to contribute a mammoth part in stemming the horrors of war or natural disasters, but nonetheless, may require the individual to attempt a small role in contributing to lessening such impact and to encourage others to participate in like constructive contribution. Success in doing so, or even in so attempting, is likely to prove a reward in itself and result in a sense of well-being. Similarly caring for others as a parent or relative or member of a social group may not of itself appear as a major contribution to humanity, but in providing both individual enjoyment as well as community benefits such activities will also be rewarding. Moreover, such successes will not depend on the priest, minister or Imam for godly praise and approval but will be recognised by the individual giver and the social benefactors.

References

Wikipedia, Eudaimonia, article, 2024
Routledge, Encyclopedia of Philosophy, The Good Life, 2024
Jim Mepham, Philosophers Explore the Good Life, Philosophy Now, 2024
Prof, Peter Adamson, Living a Good Life, Philosophy Now, 2021

Prof. Massimo Pigliucci, How to live a Happy Life, Philosophy Now, 2023
Raymond Tallis, Does the Cosmos have a Purpose?, Philosophy Now, 2024
Pinker, Steven, Enlightenment Now, Penguin, 2018.
Sam Harris, The Moral Landscape, Transworld Publishing, 2010
James Hemming, Individual Morality, 196

Hate Crime and Public Order (Scotland) Act 2022

Introduction; what the Act does

The purpose of this chapter is to examine the recently enacted law on hate crime in Scotland (2022) brought into effect in 2024. It has attracted an immense amount of criticism, most of which has been adverse; the press in general has expressed a view that the provisions undermine freedom of expression and the ability of the press and public to discuss issues related to the protected groups, as defined by race, disability and religion, inter alia, in an honest and open fashion for fear of falling foul of the new provisions. By examining the background to the provisions, the chapter attempts to throw light on what the provisions mean in reality and to promote a more informed and intelligent debate from a humanist perspective. The Act came into effect on 1 April 2024. It was passed by a 2/3 majority [82 for, 32 against and 4 abstentions] in the Scottish Parliament in 2021 and in main implemented the recommendations of a Commission headed by a retired senior judge, Lord Bracadale [Alasdair Campbell]. There was wide consultation on the report and 22 recommendations. These made no reference to the distinctions now found between race hatred crimes and other hate crimes based on the 6 identified characteristics. It rejected the extension to political, economic or social characteristics or affiliations. There has been an argument that only immutable characteristics, such as race, ethnicity, sex or disability should be included (see Grayling, 2010) but even these assumptions are questioned, sex being an example, and the case for some socially dominated beliefs, such as religion, and the vulnerability to bigotry and persecution of adherents creates a strong case for inclusion. But note also that hatred against non-believers, as a group or groups, is also included.

The Act consolidates and extends previous related provisions including those in the Public Order (Scotland) Acts, including that of 1986.
In essence, it does three things; it identifies hate expressed against identified groups as an aggravation of other crimes, it extends stirring up hatred as a separate offence and it abolishes the law on blasphemy. This note deals briefly with hate crime as a separate offence.

Section 4 of the Act states that a person commits an offence if that person behaves in a manner that a reasonable person would consider to be threatening, abusive (or insulting, for Group 1), or communicates such to another, and: -
Either
A. In doing so the person intends to stir up hatred against 1. the group identified by race, colour, nationality or ethnic or national origins or 2. the group identified by defined characteristics. These characteristics are a. age, b. disability, c. religion or perceived religious affiliation, d. sexual orientation. e. transgender identity, and f. variations in sex characteristics.
Or,
B. (for Group 1 only) a reasonable person would believe that stirring up such hatred was likely to result.
It is important to note two distinctions that the law makes between Group 1, identified by race etc. and Group 2, identified by characteristics. For the first Group 1, the offence includes 'insulting behaviour and communications' but only 'threatening or abusive behaviour and communications' applies to Group 2. Moreover, in respect of Group 2, there is the single test of the person's intention to stir up hatred and no alternative test of whether a reasonable person would believe that stirring up hatred would result (see B, above). The Humanist Society of Scotland (HSS) amongst others argued against the alternative test in submissions to government on the draft Bill when Humza Yousaf was Justice Minister.
It is a defence to the charge that the behaviour was reasonable in the particular circumstances. In determining this, particular regard should be paid to Article 10 of the ECHR relating to the importance of freedom of expression including the expression of information or ideas that offend, shock or disturb. 'Reasonable' shall be construed if there is sufficient evidence adduced to raise an issue as to whether that is the case, and the charge is not proved beyond reasonable doubt.
There is no distinction between public and private property regarding where offences may occur. This has concerned some critics regarding the potential of offences occurring at home. However given the nature of defences, the standard of proof required, and the improbability of domestic gatherings being used with the intention of stirring up hatred, the likelihood of occurrence may have seemed negligible. There was also the obvious complication of where to draw the dividing line between public and private and public and domestic which had proved an issue under the previous Race Relations and Sex legislation in the past, especially relating to 'private' clubs.

There remain practical issues relating to prosecution and enforcement. The police are overworked and undermanned in Scotland and are unlikely to consider minor offences a priority. Thus, petty theft is now given a low priority. Malicious or vexatious reporting of alleged offences is also recognised as a possibility; how well these are sifted out has yet to be tested.

It should also be recognised that there is an educational element in the legislation to promote a greater understanding, tolerance and good practice towards traditionally vulnerable groups. It remains legitimate, however, to express a controversial but honest opinion challenging. contemporary opinions or beliefs however shocking provided the intention was not to stir up hatred against a 'protected' group, or, in the case of race etc, which could reasonably be so viewed.

Complaints may be made online, by phone or in person. The police have used third-party reporting centres for a number of years. The list of centres, over 400, on the Police Scotland website, now includes a Glasgow sex shop, located near popular gay bars and nightclubs, a mushroom shop in North Berwick and a salmon and trout facility in Duns, but most are more innocuous, including housing associations and many voluntary organisations. Training is provided by the police. It is thought that the more controversial locations, as perceived by some critics, were chosen in an attempt by the police to broaden access to groups that historically have had limited or even poor links with the police, including the gay community and temporary immigrant workers.

Police Scotland intends to keep a record of hate incidents, even if they do not meet the criminal threshold. Hate crime reporting forms are available. But complaints need not be made in person nor need the complainant be identified. A large number of complaints of hatred crimes had been reported in the previous 5 years, over 5k, under the then provisions. A significant number of complaints under the Act have been ill-intentioned or vexatious including those against the then First Minister Humza Yousaf.

Conviction on a summary charge may result in a prison sentence of not more than 12 months and/or a fine, while on indictment the sentence may be up to 7 years and/or a fine.

Critics of the legislation included Russell Findlay, Conservative MSP, the historian and staunch unionist Prof. Gregory Oliver, JK Rowling, renowned author, and Ally McCoist, football commentator. While the last two have sought to be arrested for hatred offences, their conduct has failed to meet the required threshold, as yet.

Background

Articles 19 and 20 of the ICCPR

The following identifies some key elements from the report to the UN HCHR October 2008, Geneva by Agnes Callamard. This report was critical to informing the views not only of the UN but also of the member states which were signatories to the relevant convention. The media has a specific task of informing the public, she observed; it can enhance the free flow of information and ideas to individuals and communities, which in turn can help them to make informed choices for their lives. A free, independent and professional media, using investigative methods, plays a key role in providing knowledge and in giving voice to the marginalized, highlighting corruption and developing a culture of criticism where people are less apprehensive about questioning government action. So, whenever freedom of expression is unduly restricted, the realization of many other rights is attacked and undermined.

These concerns are reflected in much of the criticism of the Scottish legislation.

Article 19, UDHR and ICCPR

Freedom of expression is guaranteed under Article 19 of the Universal Declaration on Human Rights (UDHR), and more or less in similar terms under article 19 of the International Covenant on Civil and Political Rights (ICCPR): Everyone has the right to freedom of opinion and expression; this right includes the right to hold opinions without interference and to seek, receive and impart information and ideas through any media regardless of frontiers.

Freedom of expression is also protected in all three regional human rights treaties, at Article 10 of the European Convention on Human Rights (ECHR), at Article 13 of the American Convention on Human Rights and at Article 9 of the African Charter on Human and Peoples' Rights.

Yet, freedom of expression is not absolute. Both international law and most national constitutions recognise that freedom of expression may be restricted. However, any limitations must remain, it is argued, within strictly defined parameters. Article 19(3) of the ICCPR lays down the conditions with which any restriction on freedom of expression must comply.

Hate speech

International law imposes one clear positive duty upon states as far as restrictions of freedom of expression are concerned, stated in Article 20 of the UN Covenant on Civil and Political Rights – the prohibition on war propaganda and on hate speech:

"Any propaganda for war shall be prohibited by law."

"Any advocacy of national, racial or religious hatred that constitutes incitement to discrimination, hostility or violence shall be prohibited by law."

This is the only duty that States must abide by as far as restricting freedom of expression is concerned. There is, however, no agreed definition of propaganda or hate speech in international law. Instead, there are marked different regional or national approaches in restricting it. At one end of the spectrum is the US approach which protects hate speech unless (1) the speech actually incites to violence and (2) the speech will likely give rise to imminent violence. This is a very stringent standard indeed: even speech advocating violence and filled with racial insults, will be protected, if absent of a showing that violence is likely to occur, virtually immediately. At the other end of the spectrum are stringent restrictions on hate speeches, and the development of specific hate speech regulations for denying the Holocaust or other genocides. Nowhere are the substantial differences in the ways states will restrict hate speech clearer than in the European Union where countries have approached and dealt with hate groups and hate speeches with considerable variety, from the French or German position of high restriction, to that of the UK or Hungry where greater protection has been afforded to a variety of speeches.

Finding a common definition of hate speech is further complicated by the fact that the International Convention on the Elimination of Racial Discrimination (ICERD) has established a different standard, which offers the most far-reaching protections against hate speech. ICERD defines discrimination as any distinction based on race, colour, descent, or national or ethnic origin which has the purpose or effect of nullifying or impairing the enjoyment, on an equal footing, of any human right and/or fundamental freedom. States Parties are required to take a range of measures to combat discrimination, including by not engaging in discrimination, by providing effective remedies and by combating prejudice and promoting tolerance. Article 4(a) of ICERD places a specific obligation on States Parties to declare as offences punishable by law six categories of activity:

The article refers to race, colour and ethnic origin. There does not seem to be any particular logic behind the choice of these terms, and these obligations probably apply to all of the prohibited grounds of discrimination, namely race, colour, descent, and national or ethnic origin. Four of these obligations, namely (1)-(3) and (5), call for restrictions on freedom of expression.

There is no international consensus on the requirements of Article 4 and many states have entered reservations to it – all of which have the effect that the implementation of its requirements is subject to the state's own norms on the balance between freedom of expression and anti-discrimination.

As the overwhelming number of cases across the world all too well illustrates, the relationship between protecting the right to freedom of expression and resorting to criminal hate speech laws is weak. Article 19's experience to date shows that restrictions on freedom of expression, including hate-speech legislation, rarely protect against abuses, extremism, or racism. In fact, they are often used to muzzle opposition and dissenting voices, silence minorities, and reinforce the dominant political, social and moral ideology. This is especially true in periods of high-stress levels and duress, as currently and globally experienced.

In Russia, for instance, Article 282 of the Criminal Code has been applied in a discriminatory fashion and has been used to curtail freedom of expression. It is rarely applied in attacks against religious minorities by ultra-nationalist, neo-Nazi and anti-Semitic groups, instances where it could justifiably be used to safeguard democracy. This suggests selective implementation of the legislation, contrary to the requirement set out in Council of Europe Recommendation 97(20) that prosecutions be based on "objective criteria".

Hate speech laws, as with blasphemy laws, are often used by states against the very minorities they are designed to protect. In some cases, they are even used to restrict minorities from promoting their culture and identity, or from expressing concern about discrimination against them by the majority. Turkey frequently uses Article 312 of the Penal Code – which provides for up to three years' imprisonment for anybody who 'incites hatred based on class, race religion, or religious sect, or incites hatred between different regions'– against those who espouse Kurdish nationalism or even express pride in Kurdish culture. There is no evidence that censoring or banning such groups has any impact on their existence or rising influence. In fact, most evidence testifies to the fact that criminalizing such groups too often results in their radicalisation. Penalising the expression of their ideas does not reduce the problem or make the proponents of such ideas disappear.

Historically, hate speech primarily has been the prerogative of governments rather than so-called extremist groups. More usually it has been the "majority" who have exercised this against minorities or groups of the dominant culture using this against groups perceived as challenging the social order or social norms,

As noted above, Article 19 recognises that reasonable restrictions on freedom of expression may be necessary or legitimate to prevent advocacy of hatred based on nationality, race, or religion that constitutes incitement to discrimination, hostility or violence. Two key elements are involved in this standard. First, only advocacy of hatred is covered. Second, it must constitute an incitement to one of the listed results.

- In this context, "hatred" is understood to mean an irrational and intense antagonism towards an individual or group of individuals based simply on one of the listed characteristics.

- "Incitement" is understood to mean instigation or encouragement which is virtually certain to lead directly to discrimination, hostility or violence. Central to the idea of incitement is the creation of an environment where the enjoyment of the right to equality in dignity is not impossible. Incitement implies a very close link between the expression and the resulting risk of discrimination, hostility or violence, and may be distinguished, for example, from mere advocacy which supports or even calls for these results but where they are unlikely to come about.

The context is central to a determination of whether or not a given expression constitutes incitement; the likelihood of ethnic violence in the immediate aftermath of an ethnic conflict, for example, will be higher than in a peaceful, democratic environment. Any so-called hate speech restriction on freedom of expression should be carefully designed to promote equality and protect against discrimination and, as with all such restrictions, should meet the three-part test set out in Article 19 of the ICCPR (see Annex Two), according to which an interference with freedom of expression is only legitimate if:

(a) it is provided by law.

(b) it pursues a legitimate aim; and

(c) it is "necessary in a democratic society".

Specifically, any restriction should conform to the following:

- it should be clearly and narrowly defined.
- it should be applied by a body which is independent of political, commercial or other unwarranted influences, and in a manner which is

neither arbitrary nor discriminatory, and which is subject to adequate safeguards against abuse, including the right of access to an independent court or tribunal;

- no one should be penalised for statements which are true;
- no one should be criminally penalised for the dissemination of hate speech unless it has been shown that they did so with the intention of inciting discrimination, hostility or violence;
- the right of journalists to decide how best to communicate information and ideas to the public should be respected, particularly when they are reporting on racism and intolerance;
- prior censorship should not be used as a tool against hate speech;
- care should therefore be taken to apply the least intrusive and restrictive measures, in recognition of the fact that there are various available measures some of which exert less of a chilling effect on freedom of expression than others; and
- any imposition of sanctions should be in strict conformity with the principle of proportionality and criminal sanctions, in particular imprisonment, should be applied only as a last resort.

A restriction must be formulated in a way that makes clear that its sole purpose is to protect individuals holding specific beliefs or opinions, whether of a religious nature or not, from hostility, discrimination or violence, rather than to protect belief systems, religions, or institutions as such from criticism. The right to freedom of expression implies that it should be possible to scrutinise, openly debate, and criticise, even harshly and unreasonably, belief systems, opinions, and institutions, including religious ones, as long as it does not advocate hatred which incites to hostility, discrimination or violence against an individual.

All existing hate speech laws should be reviewed and amended, it is argued, as necessary to bring them into line with these standards. Consideration of new hate speech legislation should always be preceded by an analysis of whether existing legislation is in line with these standards and whether it is already sufficient to tackle the problem.

No doubt the Bracandale Report would be considered by the Scottish Government as meeting the needs of appropriate analysis.

The RABAT Plan 2012

The Rabat Plan of Action on the prohibition of advocacy of national, racial or religious hatred that constitutes incitement to discrimination, hostility or violence brings together the conclusions and recommendations from several OHCHR expert workshops (held in Geneva, Vienna, Nairobi, Bangkok and Santiago, Chile). By grounding the debate in international human rights law, the objective has been threefold:

1. To gain a better understanding of legislative patterns, judicial practices and policies regarding the concept of incitement to national, racial, or religious hatred, while ensuring full respect for freedom of expression as outlined in articles 19 and 20 of the International Covenant on Civil and Political Rights (ICCPR);
2. To arrive at a comprehensive assessment of the state of implementation of the prohibition of incitement in conformity with international human rights law and;
3. To identify possible actions at all levels.

This Plan of Action was adopted by experts at the wrap-up meeting in Rabat on 4-5 October 2012. It identified six key considerations, as follows: -

(1) Context: Context is of great importance when assessing whether particular statements are likely to incite discrimination, hostility or violence against the target group, and it may have a direct bearing on both intent and/or causation. Analysis of the context should place the speech act within the social and political context prevalent at the time the speech was made and disseminated;

(2) Speaker: The speaker's position or status in the society should be considered, specifically the individual's or organization's standing in the context of the audience to whom the speech is directed;

(3) Intent: Article 20 of the ICCPR anticipates intent. Negligence and recklessness are not sufficient for an act to be an offence under article 20 of the ICCPR, as this article provides for "advocacy" and "incitement" rather than the mere distribution or circulation of material. In this regard, it requires the activation of a triangular relationship between the object and subject of the speech act as well as the audience;

(4) Content and form: The content of the speech constitutes one of the key foci of the court's deliberations and is a critical element of incitement. Content analysis may include the degree to which the speech was provocative and direct, as well as the form, style, and nature of arguments deployed in the speech, or the balance struck between arguments deployed;

(5) Extent of the speech (or speech act): Extent includes such elements as the reach of the speech, its public nature, its magnitude and size of its audience. Other elements to consider include whether the speech is public, what means of dissemination are used, for example by a single leaflet or broadcast in the mainstream media or via the Internet, the frequency, the quantity and the extent of the communications, whether the audience had the means to act on the incitement, whether the statement (or work) is circulated in a restricted environment or widely accessible to the general public; and

(6) Likelihood, including imminence: Incitement, by definition, is an inchoate crime. The action advocated through incitement speech does not have to be committed for said speech to amount to a crime. Nevertheless, some degree of risk of harm must be identified. It means that the courts will have to determine that there was a reasonable probability that the speech would succeed in inciting actual action against the target group, recognizing that such causation should be rather direct.

The Rabat Plan notes with concern that perpetrators of incidents, which indeed reach the threshold of article 20 of the ICCPR, are not prosecuted and punished. At the same time, as we have already noted, members of minorities are de facto persecuted, with a chilling effect on others, through the abuse of vague domestic legislation, jurisprudence and policies. Political and religious leaders should refrain from using any incitement to hatred, but they also have a crucial role to play in speaking out firmly and promptly against hate speech and should make clear that violence can never be tolerated as a response to incitement to hatred.

Rabat threshold test in action

The Rabat threshold test is being used by the national authorities for audio-visual communication in Tunisia, Côte d'Ivoire and Morocco. Furthermore, in its judgment of 17 July 2018, the European Court of Human Rights referred to the Rabat Plan of Action under relevant international materials as well as in its summaries of submissions from Amnesty International, Human Rights Watch and Article 19. The United Nations peacekeeping operation in the Central African Republic is applying the Rabat test in its monitoring of incitement to violence. The UN Strategic Plan of Action on Hate Speech, which was launched in June 2019, also refers to the Rabat Plan of Action.

In August 2019, the High Commissioner addressed a Security Council meeting on advancing the safety and security of persons belonging to religious minorities in armed conflicts. In this context, she reiterated that the Rabat Plan of Action emphasizes the role of politicians and religious leaders in preventing and speaking out against intolerance, discriminatory stereotyping and instances of hate speech. In October 2021, Access Now stressed in another Arria-formula meeting that "any restriction on social media must reflect the U.N. Strategy and Plan of Action on Hate Speech and the excellent Rabat Plan of Action."

In September 2019, the OSCE Office for Democratic Institutions and Human Rights published its policy guidance on Freedom of Religion or Belief and Security. The policy guidance also encourages States to train law enforcement officials and the judiciary to understand and apply the six-part test set out in the Rabat Plan of Action to determine whether the threshold of incitement to hatred is met or not.

In his 2019 report to the General Assembly, the UN Special Rapporteur on freedom of expression recommended companies to adopt content policies that tie their hate speech rules directly to international human rights law including the Rabat Plan. While its six-part test is applicable to the criminalization of incitement, the Special Rapporteur noted that those six factors should have weight in the context of company actions against speech as well since the factors "offer a valuable framework for examining when the specifically defined content – the posts or the words or images that comprise the post – merits a restriction". In 2021, Facebook's Oversight Board referred in several decisions to the Rabat Plan of Action, using its six factors to assess the capacity of speech to create a serious risk of inciting discrimination, violence or other lawless action.

At the end of her visit to Malaysia in October 2019, the High Commissioner highlighted the Rabat Plan of Action as useful guidance in distinguishing between permissible speech and speech that may amount to incitement, and she offered the assistance of OHCHR and other UN human rights mechanisms to further explore this. In this context, the Faith for Rights framework also builds upon the Rabat Plan of Action, focussing specifically on the human rights responsibilities of faith actors. The Faith for Rights toolkit provides practical peer-to-peer learning modules, including one addressing incitement to hatred and violence in the name of religion.

The HSS Response

Freedom of speech

Humanist Society Scotland (HSS) has long advocated for clear protection of free expression within this law, especially in relation to new "stirring up" offences. While rights to freedom of speech are guaranteed by the European Convention on Human Rights (ECHR), it is important that those enforcing the law understand its limits in restricting ECHR rights. Thanks to the campaigning of the HSS, a number of major amendments were made during the passage of the bill to ensure freedom of expression was protected under the new law.

HSS still believes, Fraser Sutherland the HSS CEO advised, that the Scottish Government and Police Scotland would increase public confidence in the new act by committing to use the thresholds on hate speech set out in the Rabat Plan, as discussed above. Their use would combat much of the genuine confusion regarding the new law in practice.

However, it is also clear that much of the confusion is being deliberately manufactured by groups with an agenda, especially to undermine race and interfaith relations. For example, several individuals associated with white supremist, and ultra-nationalist groups have sought to use the implementation of this act to foment public anger against minority groups.

Recent figures from Police Scotland underline the disconnect between the hot-headed public discourse and how the law is working in practice. Of the 7,152 hate crime reports made to Police Scotland during the first week of the Act, over 3,000 were received on the first day, with numbers dropping significantly in the days after.

Fraser Sutherland, CEO, Humanist Society Scotland

Fraudulent and anonymous reporting

Figures on investigation of transgender-related hate crime are particularly interesting. Despite front-page headlines suggesting a zealous campaign against self-termed gender-critical Scots, only eight aggravated offences relating to transgender identity were deemed worthy of further police investigation. This is compared with over 120 on race, 38 on disability, and 21 on age. Moreover, it is likely, based on previous trends in this area, that most of those eight investigations will not result in charges.

From the statistics, it is surprising that a very small number of reports were made via telephone. Only 34 of the 7,152 reports were phoned in, an approach that requires the complainant to provide their name. The vast majority were received via an online form which allows anonymity.

In recent years, there has been a clear increase in toxic and degrading comments on social media platforms on issues which deserve nuanced and respectful discussion.

Humanist Society Scotland advises that it continue monitoring the enforcement of stirring-up laws by Police Scotland, in particular to ensure that ECHR rights relating to freedom of expression and belief are not undermined. But a quick look at the situation over our southern border might be instructive here. Since the introduction of stirring up offences against religion in England and Wales in 2006 there has not been a single successful prosecution in 18 years.

On occasion, inflammatory headlines tend to reduce every debate to a moralistic good against evil fallacy. The real victims of restricted freedom of expression around the world are more like Mubarak Bala, President of the Humanist Association of Nigeria, who was jailed for 24 years for a series of social media posts questioning the existence of God (HSS, April 2024).

References and Acronyms

A C Grayling, Things that Matter, Phoenix, 2010
A. Callamand, Report to the UN HCHR, 2008
Britannica online, Hate Speech, June 2024
Rabat Plan of Action, UN HRC, 2017
HSS, Humanist Society of Scotland, Press Release, April 2024
HCHR, High Commission on Human Rights
ECHR, European Convention on Human Rights
ECRI, European Commission Against Racism and Intolerance
ICCPR, International Convention on Civil and Political Rights, 1966
CERD, Committee on the Elimination of Racial Discrimination [monitors ICERD]
ICERD, Convention on the Elimination of Racial Discrimination,
OHCHR, Office of the High Commission for Human Rights
UNHRC, United Nations Human Rights Commission
UN Strategy and Plan of Action on Hate Speech, 2019
OSCE, Organisation for Security and Cooperation in Europe
Wikipedia; Entries for Hate Speech, Rabat Plan, 2024

Nationalism and the call for Independence: the UK and Scotland

What makes a nation state?

To attempt an answer to that question we might ask what is the basis of the nation state.

Clearly significant considerations may include a common language, shared history and shared culture, religion and sporting allegiance, a geographical definition of boundaries (Hutchison and Smith, 1994), ethnic identity and common aspirations (Riddoch, 2024). However, as A D Smith (1986) illustrates, none of these may be determining factors in promoting, attaining or maintaining the nation state. Moreover, many of the symbols of unity may be myths or distortions created for the purpose of promoting a sense of common identity amongst the nation's citizenry; an obvious example is the invincibility of the seafarers as depicted in 'Rule Britannia'; with successive invasions by Vikings, Romans, Saxons, Normans and Dutch [William of Orange] that notion is clearly untenable (Colley, 2014).

It may be argued that the largely monoculture of Japan, the linguistic and educational integrity of France or the colonial exploitation by the UK were critical but not shared characteristics of the respective nation states. Thus, the glue that binds different nations may not be made of the same adhesive (Smith, 1986).

The UK Experience; the constituent parts

From the thirteenth century, the Principality of Wales has conjoined with England after Edward 1 had conquered North Wales, Scotland, from the Union of the Crowns in 1603 and the union of parliaments in 1707, became Northern Britain and part of the UK. Ireland, after being subjugated to English rule first by the Anglo-Norman conquest in the 12th century by Henry 11, supposedly on religious grounds, and then by Cromwell in the 17 Century promoting the Commonwealth on like grounds, achieved independence after 1922. Northern Ireland, with its then Protestant majority, remained as part of the UK. It may be argued that the influences leading to the state of the UK, geography, conquest, a dowry, history, marriage, power, trading advantage, colonial exploitation and financial gain, amongst others were not of equal influence in the creation of the UK from its constituent parts (Colley, 2014). It may also be argued that such influences, shared or otherwise, need not be critical in maintaining the nation state or supporting continued cohesion (Smith, 1986).

However, despite the survival of a distinct Welsh language, religious adherence and, it may be argued, cultural identity, the demand for independence has been less vocal in Wales than in Scotland. Thus, clear national identity and pride in difference may not of itself demand recognition as a separate state.

Benefits and cohesion

But each part of the UK enjoyed the wealth resulting from empire, trading advantage, slavery and the industrial revolution. Glasgow, the then second city, through general commerce, tobacco, sugar, cotton and shipbuilding in particular was a beneficiary.

Electoral reforms of the nineteenth century led to fairer representation of the expanded electorate throughout the UK, and noted leaders from Wales, Ireland and Scotland as well as England played prominent roles in the British political scene in the twentieth century. The Boer War, two World Wars, rationing and reconstruction were common factors which bound the nation together. Acts of 1922 and 1928 extended the Franchise to women and economic, racial and gender disenfranchisement are not remaining issues of contention.

The inauguration of then Prince Charles as Prince of Wales, including his temporary residence in Wales and his learning the Welsh language, the Queen's heritage and love of Balmoral are symbolic factors illustrating common heritage and a shared royal family.

Post Second World War the Atlee UK government, recognised the need to provide universal support for all. Through the NHS, state pensions and unemployment benefit such measures gained common support at least among working-class people. Shared cultural interests were promoted not only through the English Proms but also through the Edinburgh Festival and Fringe and the Eisteddfod in Wales.

In Northern Ireland, with the activities of the IRA and the significant disadvantage of the Catholic minority, particularly in employment and housing, there was evident divide about being UK citizens. However, the agreement on Good Friday 1998 and the development of power sharing promised an end to the 30-year troubles. But suspension of Stormont and power sharing threatened further disunity until restored in 2024. It remains doubtful that the Irish Republic would want to assume responsibility for the troubled protestant citizenry in the north as payment for a united Ireland, even with a now Catholic majority.

UK Current Aspirations and Identity

What are the present aspirations of the UK, Scotland and the other nations? Reasonable living conditions and income, access to free and universal health, dental and care facilities, well-insulated housing with sustainable heating, education for all, employment opportunities, access to sports and recreational facilities, security and good policing, and the capacity to influence the delivery of these at a local level. The list might go on, but this demonstrates a commonality of aspiration. The question remains as to whether these are better achieved within the UK or within an independent Scotland. Moreover, the government's attitude to climate change, nuclear power and warfare as well as immigration may well influence voting intentions even if such concerns had little personal impact. From a political and economic perspective, there is also an argument about the approach. Scotland, it has been argued, might well opt for the Nordic preference for a mixed economy with greater emphasis on equality and social support than evidenced by successive UK governments.

What does Government think being British entails? Common core values and history, we are advised. Each applicant for British citizenship is asked questions about this in the context of 'Life in the UK' based on the official guide for the New Resident. Applicants are asked 24 questions and must answer 18 correctly in 45 minutes. Answers are often one of 3 or 4 options. For example, 'What is the frequency of PM questions in the House of Commons; daily, weekly or monthly? Who built the Tower of London? Where was William Shakespeare born? Who made the first minted coins in Britain?'

There are a number of issues arising from the questions? Firstly, of what relevance are they to contemporary British living? Secondly, as above examples demonstrate, few of them actually relate to Britain or the UK as a state but often relate to England alone. Applicable to those from non-English speaking states, is a test relating to understanding basic English, but not Gaelic or Welsh.

Today in the UK we may ask what the important factors are that support the concept of 'UK and British Nationality' and which factors pull the nation apart; and with what consequence.

We are advised that basic UK values include freedom of expression and association, commitment to democratic elections and in the separation of powers between the executive, or government, the legislature, or parliament, and the judiciary. Not least, is our adherence to international norms relating to equality, justice, free speech and freedom from torture and maltreatment. While the UK has no written constitution, the Bill of Right, for England and Wales and the Claim of Right for Scotland along with the concept of Habeas Corpus enshrine some expectation of accountability for governance and the judicial system. It is true, however, that a simple Act of Parliament can strip such rights without constraint. The proposal to obviate the decisions of the Human Rights Court under the European Convention by making the UK Supreme Court the last appeal body is a case in point.

But, the Equality Act 2010, the Humans Rights Act 1998, and related provision relating to the protection of fair treatment for employees, for consumers, for tenants, for patients and for citizens generally are designed to promote and protect essential citizen wellbeing. Similarly, the accountability of public life, from the prison service to the police to local and central governance, give a veneer if not exactly a reality to protection from abuse by the powerful.

With the creation of devolved power to the Scottish Parliament, the Welsh Assembly and to Stormont such rights and obligations are often protected and enforced at the national level, although frequently under the guidance of the mother of parliaments, The creation of Mayors in strategic locations in England further demonstrate devolution of power and responsibility to a local level.

All is well in the state of Denmark, Nordic Noir excepting; or is it?

Scotland and Nationhood:

For

What is it that now questions the value of the UK state to Scotland? Historically, the exploitation of UK, or Scotland's oil, to the predominant benefit of England, in proportional terms rankled many, but the failure to create a national benefit from the income, compared to the Norway for example, was more irksome. In the Thatcher years Scotland was characterised as a UK region and a poll tax guinea pig. A further factor of alienation.

Similarly, the decision to leave the EU was achieved through a UK majority vote but with less than 40% support from Scottish voters.; While the SNP dominated Scottish Parliament wished EU re-admittance, the Tories and Labour Party were not so persuaded.

The location of a nuclear weapons base at Holy Loch has remained contentious and the argument for independence is that it should be removed. Indeed, the predominant view in Scotland is that the country, whether Scotland or the UK, should no longer aspire to be party to top table discussions, as supposed equals with China, Russia, the USA and India. Similarly, it's membership of the UN Security Council is questionable. It should spend a greater proportion of its income on the NHS, social services and welfare support as well as education and housing rather than defence. The problems resulting from Brexit relating to scientific cooperation, student exchanges, residence, health insurance, passport and visa controls, common immigration issues and policing, amongst others are only solvable with much greater cooperation with Europe as enabled by the EU and the single market. Issues the new Labour government may attempt to ameliorate.

However, an independent Scotland, it is argued, would be much better placed to identify its own priorities. The postwar dominance of the Conservative Party and its commitment to trickle down Friedman economics would be at an end. The deluge of privatisation would be challenged; while a mixed economy which valued private enterprise might continue, the lost Labour ideal of controlling the heights of the economy and of central interest to national well-being such as water, the railways and integrated public transport, the NHS and Social Care and housing would be coordinated for the public good. In respect of cultural activities, it has been argued, that, as with Paris and the French desert (14), the stifling predominance of London and the Southeast would be contested, and a reinvigorated Scottish art and culture scene allowed to flourish.

Against

The arguments against independence are also compelling and some challenge the assumptions articulated above. Would we not be better placed in the UK as members of the G7 and G20 as well as the UN Security Council to promote and protect our shared interests?

The Barnet Formula on which the allocation of financial resources to Scotland is based and which results in a greater per capita allocation than to England, would be lost. Indeed, the resource from estimated income of an independent Scotland would be less, unless and until the growth envisaged by the SNP was realised. With 60% of Scottish trade exports going to England, special deals would have to be negotiated. Issues relating to pensions, residence, citizenship, currency and the national debt, amongst others would have to be resolved (6).

Moreover, an independent Scotland does not equate with regional satisfaction within Scotland. Recently Orkney and Shetland have debated the value of a return to Denmark or becoming part of Norway, reflecting some concern about their treatment by the Scottish devolved Government. The fiasco concerning the Scottish Government contract for new ferries to serve the West Coast and the Scottish Islands does not portray a unity of view regarding priorities or competence in serving more outlying areas. Indeed, the pollution of Scottish Rivers by Scottish Water and problems relating to Scottish Rail suggests that the nationalisation of key activities or their close control by governance does not promise an easy solution through an independent state.

Dominant Concerns

Scotland as with the rest of the UK was heavily involved in the slave trade. Through colonial activities it also collected and maintains many artefacts purloined at that time. Restitution when agreed would have to be apportioned between the UK and Scotland. No doubt a cause of much dispute and wrangling.

Given the evidence of climate change illustrated by the fires raging in Greece, Italy, Croatia and Spain and the USA in the summer of 2023 and in California and Canada amongst other countries in 2024 as well as the floods experienced in India, Bangladesh and SE Asia, and the UK, the world must address the action agreed at an international level as a matter of urgency. While international action is necessary, steps towards this at regional level may prove a leaver to encourage and inspire change. Unfortunately, the UK government has already bowed to political pressure to renege on many of its undertakings, but would an independent Scottish Government prove more resolute and, if so, more influential in promoting wider interest and, crucially, activity?

Another concern is illustrated by the divisions over Brexit. While differences in the degree of support or lack of it were manifested in the votes returned in England, Wales, Northern Ireland and Scotland as well as regional differences, illustrated by London voting in favour of remain, it is of significance to note that opinions of the young were also in favour of remaining; it is they who will inherit responsibility for implementing decisions with which they disagree. It is also relevant to note that in Scotland the minority ethnic population, those classified as working class and the Catholic minority were also in favour of independence (10). In addition, it is clear that a significant number of voters have changed their minds in the light of the problems now manifest but perhaps hidden at the time, even deliberately so. It is also apparent that there was considerable dishonesty in promoting the leave as well as the remain campaigns.

Whose Decision?

But of what relevance is this to a vote on independence? Again, the young will inherit the responsibility for implementation, arguments pro and anti are likely to be exaggerated and, importantly, attitudes may change over time in the light of the practical consequences of the decision. This would suggest two considerations. Firstly, that a weighting should be given to those younger voters, say 40 years and younger, and second that the margin should be substantial. While many objected to the substantial vote required for devolution under the first Scotland Act, devolution was a reversible decision while independence is not, at least in the shorter term. Accordingly, a weighted majority of say 60% might be a sensible precaution.

One of the problems associated with the continuing plea for a second referendum on independence is that the pro campaign will continue to press for referenda until a decision is favourable; while this is logical from the pro faction, it may seem exhausting of time and money from those in opposition. Again, a weighted majority might defer demand until a fairly substantial majority in favour of a pro vote was manifest.

While the Humanist would favour democratic decision-making and might recognise the democratic deficit under the present system, the moral argument for independence is not clear-cut, as the above has sought to make evident. That said, it would seem contentious to challenge such a decision when made by a substantial majority; an unlikely eventuality in the shorter term. The Amsterdam Humanist Declaration of 1952, as amended in Glasgow in 2022 is unequivocal in its opposition to authoritarian nationalism and tribal sectarianism. There is no doubt that the SNP would point to both its membership and its policy of embracing all denizens of Scotland as citizens in the new state to deny any evidence of tribal exclusion or sectarianism. It is true, however, that a minority expressed its support for the referendum in an aggressive manner, intimidating legitimate opposition. Some have also accused the SNP leadership to be clannish and exclusionary under both Salmon and Sturgeon. Moreover, the financial misappropriation alleged within the SNP, still under police inquiry, raised serious questions concerning transparency. Such attitudes and behaviour require to be challenged, perhaps more vigorously than in the past. It may be surprising that, despite such challenges to SNP leadership as evidenced by the very substantial swing to Labour in the 2024 Westminster elections, the support for independence has not diminished substantially.

Increased devolved powers remained a possibility after the 'No' vote in 2014. Within the Nordic region, there is a much more relaxed attitude to constitutional change, in contrast with the confrontational approach in the UK. Thus, after Brexit, Theresa May contemptuously rejected attempts to achieve a Scottish opt out while preparing deals for Car manufacturers and East Anglian Farmers. In like manner, Rishi Sunak failed to consult any devolved constituents before radically altering the 'green' timetable in 2023.

It is argued that had Scotland been a constituent part of Denmark or Norway the case for a differentiated settlement would have been more readily achieved with the option of becoming a member of EFTA and the single market through the EEC a reality which would have weakened the case for a further referendum because of Brexit.

The problem with increasing devolved powers is that it does not address the central issue of unfettered control by Westminster; power devolved is power retained. Nor does it obviate the contradictions inherent in the present distribution of power. The first issue is illustrated by the suspension of decision making by Stormont in Northern Ireland which results in reinstating decision making in Westminster until 2024. Moreover, some of the powers applying to the UK through the Common Agricultural Policy (CAP) were retained by Westminster rather than devolved, as deemed equitable, to the Scottish Parliament. A constitutional and unequivocal allocation of responsibility to the Stormont parliament would deny the option of the withdrawal from power sharing in the sense that the remaining party or parties would then exercise full responsibility for devising and implementing decisions.

A Third Way and the Balance of Power?

There is little escaping a radical constitutional change which involves a written constitution and possibly the creation of a federal system.

A number of institutions, the Liberal Democrats and politicians, notably Gordon Brown, have called for a third way, a federal structure or, as Gordon Brown describes it, a voluntary multinational association . As we have noted, if the SNP goal of independence is achieved, there will be problems relating to defence, currency, taxation, pensions, investment, trading arrangements, foreign policy, fuel and power and the green agenda, to name a few. A particular advantage of the federal approach is that existing arrangements, so far as beneficial and agreed upon, may be continued. A particular disadvantage is that some of the more contentious issues such as foreign policy, war and human rights and international conventions and treaties, nuclear deterrence and taxation will require to be resolved.

In determining the power to be provided to a federal government, there are many examples to choose from for consideration, but to protect the legitimate concern of those in favour of independence, there has to be a mechanism for enabling relative autonomy in respect of taxation for state purposes and for priorities in respect of expenditure such as the state NHS, housing, human rights and equality, employment and social welfare.

Critical issues relate to decision-making and the balance of power relating to foreign policy and warfare; any approach which diminishes the fundamental integrity of individual states i.e. England, Scotland, Wales and Northern Ireland should be resisted. Given the significance to all states, such decisions may have to be determined by a 3 of 4 majority of states. Obviously, England with three quarters of the population would have difficulty with an approach which assigns equal responsibility to members of a federal system. However, this may be a price worth paying if the UK Government preferred a federal solution to a total break up. It should also be borne in mind that the income derived in England from personal taxation and VAT, from company tax and inheritance tax, for example, would be commensurate with their larger population. It should be recognised that regional and national inequalities have undermined the lives of millions cut off from a better future reflected in shorter lives, worse health, lower wages and fewer educational opportunities . Today London and SE attract 72% of new R&D intensive jobs and 45% of private investment. It enjoys double the infrastructure spend per head in the UK.

There is a concern in England, in particular, about regional power and devolved autonomy. It seems sensible for such concerns to be addressed by individual states and not to be part of any federal settlement; devolution within an integral state would be for the state concerned to decide and this may change over time. Thus, England might decide that Cornwall, Yorkshire and Lancashire should be afforded devolved authority while Scotland might consider Shetland and Orkney and/or the Inner Hebrides be devolved. Such arrangements would allow member states to have constitutional responsibility to effect changes as they deem fit.

The recent report by the Labour Party (the Brown Commission, previously alluded to) attempted to analyse the current constitutional malaise and concluded with six sets of recommendations. These included the abolition of the House of Lords and increased powers allocated to the UK nations and the 'Regions'. The issues not addressed were the creation of an English Parliament by reforming the House of Commons, the means of creating a truly federal structure in a new constitution and the allocation of appropriate power to the nations to conclude agreements relating to EFTA and the EEC, as allowed to the Faroes by Denmark, for example. How and if, the Labour Government will address these proposals is awaited!

And More

It may be preferable, in contrast to the proposals, for the House of Commons to have the responsibility of the English State alone. The federal body, say comprising 20 MPs from each state, might sit in each state on a rotating basis as an Assembly of the Nations.

As far as the monarchy is concerned, and recognising the support for the notion 'Not our King' and well as the Humanist support for an elected head of state, each state as a member of the federal structure might then agree on the process for appointing/electing a constitutional Head its of its own state, if thought necessary, and jointly of the Federal Government with only ceremonial and possibly advisory powers. The lands and properties owned by the crown would become owned by respective states with responsibility for maintenance, through income and expenditure.

Trade, with Brexit and the Scottish preference for remaining in the EU, is clearly a problem. One outcome which may be welcomed by many in all states would be the compromise of the federal government joining EFTA and the EEA but only if such trading arrangements were not allocated to the member states. This would enable participation in the single market but avoid the problems associated with of the Federation seeking to rejoin the EU. The Labour Government has already proposed a strengthening of EU ties.

This would also help solve the issue of Northern Ireland trade borders and preserve the integrity of the Sunning-dale and Good Friday agreements. Again, negotiations with Northern Ireland and the Republic would be essential.

A significant hurdle to the promotion of a truly federal UK state is that the largest component, namely England, and more particularly the House of Commons and their elected members, won't wear it. This is primarily for two reasons.

Firstly from 1707 and the Union of the Scottish and English Parliaments with their location in Westminster, London, the weight of MPs, their voting power and their influence has been such that the UK parliament, despite Scottish, Irish and Welsh representation, has been viewed as English and both the House of Commons and House of Lords are commonly viewed as part of the English establishment. Symbolically, God Save the King is not the UK anthem, but the English anthem played without irony or apology to other constituent nations. Consequently, there is an avowed sense of both ownership and leadership emanating from this weighty majority so much so that any challenging claim of an equal or legitimate entitlement to question such ascendancy is often treated with condescension if not derision, as exemplified by the refusal of Liz Truss in 2022, after her appointment as Prime Minister, to meet The First Minister, with the added insult that the First Minister was told by Truss to be attention seeking. Another example, as previously noted, is that of Rishi Sunak arbitrary changing the timetable relating to climate change without consultation with any of the devolved governments (30 October, 2023, The 'I'). However, Starmer, soon after assuming office as PM, met the devolved heads of state including Sweeney, and despite the Labour Party opposing independence, a more engaging relationship with the devolved nations may eventuate. Unfortunately, the UK government's decision, without consultation, to slash a return to the old ways.

Secondly with the existing system, despite acknowledged imperfections, securing such dominance of the English majority, the need for reform of any kind, particularly resulting in leakage of power and patronage, is largely unattractive to the English dominance. This may be the reason for the Brown Commission to advocate regional change simultaneously with national federalism to seduce otherwise recalcitrant support. Consequently, despite its evident appeal to securing a better future for member states, a federal structure will prove unpalatable to both Houses.

A Conclusion

This being the likely outcome of testing a meaningful reform towards a federal structure, the well-articulated case for independence will be substantially reinforced and the resurgence of the labour vote in Scotland, as demonstrated by the Westminster elections of 2024, possibly a temporary but undoubtedly challenging impediment to independence. Meanwhile, however, it seems probable that the existing constitutional arrangements will limp on and, at most, piecemeal reform by any government in Westminster is the most that can be expected. The SNP/Green association, after the formal alliance was terminated by the then First Minister, Humza Yusuf, will be challenged and the competence of the SNP in government questioned further in the 2026 Holyrood election, which, however unrelated to the separatist voice, may well undermine the case for radical change let alone independence. The curse may comprise the resultant disillusionment of the Scottish electorate. The UK electorate had expressed disillusionment with government both north and south of the border. The spectre of right-wing authoritarian leadership filling the vacuum with the rise of Nigel Farage's Reform Party seemingly replicating the success of the likes of Giorgia Meloni in Italy has been counterbalanced by the size of the Labour Party Majority in the 2024 elections. However, the continuing threat of Trump and the neo-liberal leaders in Europe looms large. The future for independence for Scotland in a social, caring and democratic state appears under significant threat as does the creation of a truly federal structure with a written constitution and reform of both Houses in a cohesive, co-operative and cogent UK state, perhaps even further distant.

Nationalism; selected Bibliography

Linda Colley, ' Acts of Union and Disunion', Profile Books, 2014
Anthony Smith 'The Ethnic Origin of Nations', Basil Blackwell, 1986
Lesley Riddoch and Eberhart Bort, 'McSmorgasbord', Luath Press, 2017
Lesley Riddoch, Thrive; the freedom to flourish, Viewpoint, 2024
John Hutchison and Anthony Smith, 'Nationalism', Oxford Readers, Oxford University Press, 1994
Nigel Warburton, The Worrying link over cruelty to Animals, The New European, Nov. 2021
Tim Marshall, ' Prisoners of Geography', Elliot and Thompson, 2015.
Gavin McCrone ' Scottish Independence; Weighing up the economics', Birlinn Ltd, 2013
Minority Rights Group.'World Directory of Minorities', MRG International, 1997
Scottish Government, 'Building a New Scotland', [Constitution and democracy, Economy, Money and Tax] 2022; one of series setting out Governments proposals for an Independent Scotland.
Tom Nairn, 'The Break-up of Britain', Verso, Revised Edition, 2021
T.M. Devine, 'Independence or Union', Penguin, 2017

T.M. Devine, 'The Scottish Nation', Penguin. 2012

Gordon Donaldson, 'Scotland; The Shaping of a Nation', David and Charles, 1980.

Wikipedia, under 1. Scottish Nationalism, 2. Unionism, 3. Scottish Independence, and 4. Scottish Republicanism.

J.F. Gravier 'Paris and the French Desert', 1947

'A New Britain', Report of the Commission, Chaired by Gordon Brown, on the UK's Future, July 2023.

The Social Contract

Introduction

This chapter seeks to outline the basic precepts underpinning the idea of the 'social contract' with particular reference to Hobbes, Locke, and Rousseau, the important developers of the idea, and Rawls and Sens whose writings are of contemporary relevance in both legal and social philosophy.

The importance of the social contract is that it may be seen to define the relationship of the citizen and community to the state, or monarch or even dictator. To some the contract was seen as an absolute conveyance or concession of power and authority to the ruler/s, however defined, in exchange for security and safety in respect of life and limb. For others the contract was conditional on the ruler/s not only providing such security and safety but also providing a government to the demonstrable well-being of the community as well as the individual citizen. In Scotland the Declaration of Arbroath of 1320, the Treatise by the humanist George Buchanan in 1579 (De Jure Regni Apud Scotus) and the Claim of Right of 1689 all qualified the doctrine of the divine right of kings and promoted the idea of a tacit contract between the ruler and the ruled. In the instance of the last, it was argued that the king's breach of contract justified the declaration that James V11 had forfeited the throne as his actions had violated his legal and constitutional duties (see Articles of Grievances).

In 2019 the Claim, as affirmed by the Scottish Act of Union of 1707, was cited by MPs when successfully seeking a ruling that the prorogation of Parliament by Boris the Bad was unlawful.

In the run up to the 2024 July Westminster election, Nigel Farage, the leader of the Reform Party, made explicit reference to a social contract between his party and the electorate; this description was in preference to the various manifestos offered by the other parties. It may be that a 'binding' contract is more readily offered when there is no prospect of the party concerned being elected to govern, and therefore held to account!

Accordingly, while no explicit 'social contract' may exist in the UK or indeed in Scotland, the concept may retain some contemporary relevance in defining and qualifying the relationship between the monarchy and the government and the government and the citizen and community. To the Humanist there is clearly no divine right to govern and there is no written constitution. As a result, any tacit contract may be seen as fluid and negotiable. But on what basis? The following may provide a framework for such discussion.

Historical Origins

The social contract is seen as an actual or hypothetical compact, or agreement, between the ruled or between the ruled and their rulers, defining the rights and duties of each. In primeval times, according to the theory, individuals were born into an anarchic natural state, and were happy or unhappy according to the particular version of the theory is applied. They then, by exercising reason and self-interest, formed a community and government by means of a social contract.

While similar ideas can be traced to the Greek Sophists, social contract theories had their greatest currency in the 17th and 18th centuries and are associated with the English philosophers Thomas Hobbes and John Locke and the Genevan philosopher Jean-Jacques Rousseau. What distinguished these theories of political obligation from other doctrines of the period was their attempt to justify and delimit political authority on the grounds of individual self-interest and rational consent.

The advantages of organized government when compared with the disadvantages of the perceived state of nature, showed why and under what conditions government is useful and ought therefore to be accepted by all reasonable people as a voluntary obligation. These conclusions were then reduced to the form of a social contract, from which it was supposed that all the essential rights and duties of citizens could be logically deduced. [see entries in Encyclopaedia Britannica online for extended discussion].

The social contract in Hobbes

In Hobbes (Leviathan, 1651), the natural state provided no enforceable criteria of right and wrong. People only looked after themselves as individuals and took all that they could; life was "solitary, poor, nasty, brutish and short." The state of nature was a state of conflict, which could be ended only if individuals agreed by way of a social contract to give their liberty into the hands of a sovereign, on the sole condition that their lives were safeguarded by sovereign power.

For Hobbes the authority of the sovereign is absolute. His will is law and not subject to challenge. That said, subjects remain free to act as they please in cases in which the sovereign is silent (in other words, when the law does not address the action concerned). The social contract allows individuals to leave the state of nature and enter civil society, but the former remains a threat and returns as soon as governmental power collapses. Because the power of Leviathan the political state is uncontested. However, its collapse is very unlikely and occurs only when it is no longer able to protect its subjects.

The social contract in Locke

Locke differed from Hobbes in the second of the two Treaties of Government, 1690, insofar as he conceived of the state of nature as a state in which humans, though free, equal, and independent, are obliged under the natural law to respect each other's rights to life, liberty, and property. Individuals, however, agree to leave the state of nature to form a commonwealth in order to institute an impartial power capable of arbitrating disputes and redressing injuries. Accordingly, Locke held that the obligation to obey civil government under the social contract was conditional upon the protection of the natural rights of each person, including the right to private property. Kings and Governments who violated these terms could be justifiably overthrown.

Locke thus stated that there can be no subjection to power without consent, even if tacit, though once political society has been founded, citizens are obligated to accept the decisions of a majority of their number. Such decisions are made on behalf of the majority by the legislature, though the ultimate power of choosing the legislature rests with the people. The powers of the legislature are not absolute, because the law of nature remains as a permanent standard and as a principle of protection against arbitrary authority.

The social contract in Rousseau

Jean-Jaques Rousseau, in his *Discourse on the Origin of Inequality, 1755*, held that in the state of nature humans were solitary but also healthy, happy, good, and free. What Rousseau called "nascent societies" were formed when people began to live together as families and neighbours; that development, however, gave rise to negative and destructive passions such as jealousy and pride, which in turn fostered social inequality and human vice. The introduction of private property marked a further step toward inequality since it made law and government necessary as a means of protecting it. Rousseau regretted the "fatal" concept of property and the "horrors" that resulted from the departure from a condition in which the earth belonged to no one.

In the *Discourse*, civil society, as Rousseau described it, was created for two purposes: to provide peace for everyone and to ensure the right to property for anyone lucky enough to have possessions. It was thus of some advantage to everyone, but mostly to the advantage of the rich, since it transformed their de facto ownership into rightful ownership and kept the poor dispossessed. It was, indeed, a somewhat biased social contract, since the poor got so much less out of it than did the rich.

The Social Contract, the Principles of Political Right 1762, comprised 4 parts with the opening salvo 'Man is born free but is everywhere in chains'.

a] Foundations of Legitimate Political Order
b] Origins and Functions of the Sovereign Body
c] the role of Government
d] Issues regarding a just society

This attempted to outline how to establish legitimate authority in a political community compatible with individual freedom in the face of a commercial society. The following are key elements.

1. Only the General Will of the Populace [as agreed by all adult members of the relevant community] has the right to legislate; no divine right of kings.
2. Might is not right. In a civil society, morality reflects the will of the people.
3. Government must be effected with the consent of the people- the social contract- and not threaten individual civil freedoms which would be protected by the   state. Such consent, it is argued, is largely implicit and civil freedom are distinguished from 'natural' freedoms- those of the unlicensed "noble savage"
4. Laws must apply equally to all
5. Laws should preserve [promote] equality
6. The Sovereign must not exercise executive power and is subject to the will of the people which might legitimately remove a sovereign.
7. The populace should exercise direct power rather than through representative democracy [clearly influenced by Geneva and referendums]
8. States should be small enough to make such governance possible.
9. Religion/the church should not play a dominant role in governance.

Rousseau believed in the possibility of a genuine social contract, one in which people would receive in exchange for their independence a better kind of freedom, namely true political, or republican, liberty. As described in *Du Contrat Social* (1762; such liberty is to be found in obedience to what Rousseau called the *volonté générale* (the "general will")—a collectively held will that aims at promoting the common good or the common interest.

Rousseau's idea of citizenship was much more organic and much less individualistic than Locke's. The surrender of independence, or natural liberty, for political liberty meant that all individual rights, including rights in property, are subordinate to the general will. For Rousseau the state is a moral entity whose life is the union of its members, whose laws are acts of the general will, and whose end is the liberty and equality of its citizens. It follows that when any government usurps the power of the people, the social contract is broken; and not only are the citizens no longer compelled to obey, but they may also, in extremis, have an obligation to rebel.

Many social contract theorists, including Hobbes, recognized that their concepts of the social contract and the state of nature were not historically based and that they could be justified only as a hypothesis useful for the clarification of a timeless political problem relating to governance.

The Social Contract in Rawls

John Rawls' in his A Theory of Justice 1971, advances the concept of 'justice as fairness' which advocates equal basic liberties, equality of opportunity, and facilitating the maximum benefit to the least advantaged members of society in any case where inequalities may occur. Rawls uses a hypothesis he calls the 'original position', in which people consciously select what kind of society they would choose to live in if they did not know which social position they would personally occupy. In his later work, Political Realism (1993), Rawls turned to the question of how political power could be made legitimate given reasonable disagreement about the nature of the good life. His essential notion is to seek judgment of fairness for all assuming the *Original position*; in which, everyone decides principles of justice from behind a veil of ignorance. This "veil" is one that essentially blinds people to all facts about themselves so they cannot tailor principles to their own advantage:

No one knows his place in society, his class position or social status, nor does anyone know his fortune in the distribution of natural assets and abilities, his intelligence, strength, and the like. I shall even assume that the parties do not know their conceptions of the good or their special psychological propensities. The principles of justice are chosen behind a veil of ignorance.

Rawls posits two basic capacities that individuals would know themselves to possess. First, individuals know that they have the capacity to form, pursue and revise a conception of the good, or life plan. Exactly what sort of conception of the good this is, however, the individual does not yet know. It may be, for example, religious or secular, but at the start, the individual in the original position does not know which. Second, each individual understands themselves to have the capacity to develop a sense of justice and a generally effective desire to abide by it. Knowing only these two features of themselves, the group will deliberate in order to design a social structure, during which each person will seek their maximal advantage. The idea is that proposals that we would ordinarily think of as unjust—such as that black people or women should not be allowed to hold public office—will not be proposed, in this, Rawls's original position, because it would be *irrational* to propose them. The reason is simple: one does not know whether he himself would be a woman or a black person. This position is expressed in the difference principle, according to which, in a system of ignorance about one's status, one would strive to improve the position of the worst off, because he might find himself in that position.

Rawls models his original position after the "initial situations" of various social contract thinkers including the three preceding, Hobbes, Locke and Rousseau as described above. Each constructs their initial situation somewhat differently, having in mind a unique political morality which they intend the thought experiment to generate. Rawls also acknowledges the influence of both David Hume and Immanuel Kant in evaluating justice and fairness. Ian King has suggested the original position draws on Rawls's experiences in post-war Japan, where the US Army was challenged with designing new social and political authorities for the country, while "imagining away all that had gone before."

In social justice processes, each person early on makes decisions about which features of persons to consider and which to ignore. Rawls's aspiration is to have created a thought experiment whereby a version of that process is carried to its completion, illuminating the correct standpoint a person should take in their thinking about justice. If he has succeeded, then the original position thought experiment may function as a full specification of the moral standpoint we should attempt to achieve when deliberating about social justice.

In setting out his theory, Rawls described his method as one of "Reflective equilibrium' a concept which has since been used in other areas of philosophy. Reflective equilibrium is achieved by mutually adjusting one's general principles and one's considered judgements on particular cases, to bring the two into line with one another.

The core of Political Liberalism is its insistence that in order to retain its legitimacy, the liberal state must commit itself to the "ideal of public reason." This roughly means that citizens in their public capacity must engage one another only in terms of reasons whose status *as* reasons is shared between them. Political reasoning, then, is to proceed purely in terms of "public reasons." For example: a US Supreme Court Justice deliberating on whether or not the denial to homosexuals of the ability to marry constitutes a violation of the 14th Amendment's Equal Protection Clause may not refer to his religious convictions on the matter, but he may take into account the argument that a same-sex household provides sub-optimal conditions for a child's development. This is because reasons based upon the interpretation of sacred text are non-public (their force as reasons rely upon faith commitments that can be reasonably rejected), whereas reasons that rely upon the value of providing children with environments in which they may develop optimally are public reasons—their status as reasons draws upon no deep, controversial conception of human flourishing.

Rawls held that the duty of civility—the duty of citizens to offer one another reasons that are mutually understood as rational—applies within what he called the "public political forum." This forum extends from the upper reaches of government—for example the supreme legislative and judicial bodies of the society—all the way down to the deliberations of a citizen deciding for whom to vote in state legislatures or how to vote in public referendums. Campaigning politicians should also, he believed, refrain from pandering to the non-public religious or moral convictions of their constituencies.

The publicly agreed political values—freedom, equality, and fairness- serve as the foundation of the liberal state. As any justification for these values would necessarily draw upon deep (religious or moral) commitments which could be denied socially, Rawls held that public political values may only be justified privately by individual citizens. This clearly appears a contradiction in terms, but he contends that these public liberal values may and will be affirmed publicly (in judicial opinions and presidential addresses, for example) but its deep justifications will not. Thus, a reasonable Catholic will justify the liberal values one way while a reasonable Muslim another, and a reasonable secular citizen yet another way. This is Rawls's notion of an "overlapping consensus."

Rawls; Influence and reception

Rawls's writings have exerted an enormous impact on not only contemporary moral and political philosophy but also public political discourse. During the Tiananmen Square protests in 1989, copies of "A Theory of Justice" were brandished by protesters in the face of government officials. Despite being approximately 600 pages long, over 300,000 copies of that book have been sold, stimulating critical responses from a wide variety of critics including many scholars.

Although having a profound influence on his work, both in theory and in practice, the generally anti-meritocratic sentiment of Rawls's analysis has not been widely accepted by the political left. He consistently held the view that naturally developed skills and endowments could not be neatly distinguished from inherited ones, and that neither could be used to justify moral worth. Instead, he held the view that individuals could "legitimately expect" entitlements to the earning of income or development of abilities based on institutional arrangements. This aspect of Rawls's work has been instrumental in the development of such ideas as luck egalitarianism and the concept of unconditional basic income, which have themselves been criticized. The strictly egalitarian quality of Rawls's second principle of justice has called into question the type of equality that fair societies ought to embody.

In a 2008 national survey of political theorists, based on 1,086 responses from professors at accredited, four-year colleges and universities in the United States, Rawls was voted first on the list of "Scholars Who Have Had the Greatest Impact on Political Theory in the Past 20 Years".

Social Contract in Amartya Sen

In *Development as Freedom*, Sen outlines five specific types of freedoms: political freedoms, economic facilities, social opportunities, transparency guarantees, and protective security. Political freedoms refer to the ability of the people to have a voice in government and to be able to scrutinize the authorities. Economic facilities concern both the resources within the market and the market mechanism itself. Any focus on income and wealth in the country would serve to increase the economic facilities for the people. Social opportunities deal with the establishments that provide benefits like healthcare or education for the populace, allowing individuals to live better lives. Transparency guarantees allow individuals to interact with some degree of trust and knowledge of the interaction. Protective security is the system of social safety nets that prevent a group affected by poverty being subjected to terrible misery. Before Sen's work, these had been viewed as only the ends of development; luxuries afforded to countries that focus on increasing income. However, Sen argues that the increase in real freedoms should be both the ends and the means of development. He elaborates upon this by illustrating the closely interconnected natures of the five main freedoms as he believes that the expansion of one of those freedoms can lead to expansion in another one as well. In this regard, he discusses the correlation between social opportunities of education and health and how both of these complement economic and political freedoms as a healthy and well-educated person is better suited to make informed economic decisions and be involved in fruitful political demonstrations etc. A comparison is also drawn between China and India to illustrate this interdependence of freedoms. Both countries were working towards developing their economies, China since 1979 and India since 1991.

Welfare economics seeks to evaluate economic policies in terms of their effects on the well-being of the community. Sen, who devoted his career to such issues, was called the "conscience of his profession". His influential monograph *Collective Choice and Social Welfare* (1970), which addressed problems related to individual rights (including formulation of the liberal paradox), justice and equity, majority rule, and the availability of information about individual conditions, inspired researchers to turn their attention to issues of basic welfare. Sen devised methods of measuring poverty that yielded useful information for improving economic conditions for the poor. For instance, his theoretical work on inequality provided an explanation for why there are fewer women than men in India and in China despite the fact that in the West and in poor but medically unbiased countries, women have lower mortality rates at all ages, live longer, and make a slight majority of the population. Sen claimed that this skewed ratio results from the better health treatment and childhood opportunities afforded boys in those countries, as well as sex-selective abortions.

Governments and international organisations handling food crises were influenced by Sen's work. His views encouraged policy makers to pay attention not only to alleviating immediate suffering but also to finding ways to replace the lost income of the poor—for example through public works—and to maintain stable prices for food. A vigorous defender of political freedom, Sen believed that famines do not occur in functioning democracies because their leaders must be more responsive to the demands of the citizens. In order for economic growth to be achieved, he argued, social reforms—such as improvements in education and public health—must precede economic reform. In 2009, Sen published 'The Idea of Justice'. Based on his previous work in welfare economics and social choice theory, but also on his philosophical thoughts, Sen presented his own theory of justice that he meant to be an alternative to the influential modern theories of justice of John Rawls in particular. In opposition to Rawls but also earlier justice theoreticians Kant, Rousseau or Hume, and inspired by the philosophical works of Adam Smith and Mary Wollstonecraft, Sen developed a theory that is both comparative and practical (instead of being transcendental and institutional). However, he still regards institutions and processes as being equally important. As an alternative to Rawls's veil of ignorance, Sen chose the though experiment of an impartial spectator as the basis of his theory of justice. He also stressed the importance of public discussion and a focus on people's capabilities, including the notion of universal human rights, in evaluating various states with regard to justice.

He referred to 'rational economic man' as motivated mainly by self-interest. He points out that children have strong notions of fairness and acute aversion to manifest injustice. In his introduction to *The Idea of Justice*, Sen states that the strong perception of manifest injustice applies to adult human beings as well as children. What moves us is not the realization that the world falls short of being completely just – which few of us expect – but that there are clearly remediable injustices around us which we want to eliminate.

Thus, Sen asserts that human beings are as concerned with eliminating remediable injustice as they are with pursuing their own self-interest.

However, since human beings have an innate desire to eliminate injustice where possible, institutions are not that important. Ideal institutions are not required to inculcate a sense of fairness or to persuade people to act fairly or to police them very strictly so as to prevent anti-social behaviour. Since ideal institutions aren't necessary and since people have an innate desire to eliminate remediable injustice, it follows that 'Public Reason'—i.e., open discussion and rational argument—can enable what Sen calls 'plural grounding', this being an 'overlapping consensus' (in Rawls's terminology) between people of different ideologies or belief or value systems such that people can agree upon comparative evaluations regarding justice without having to agree about all their values and beliefs.

One of Sen's main arguments is that the project of social justice should not be evaluated in binary terms, as either achieved or not. Rather, he claims that justice should be understood as existing to a matter of degree and should correspondingly be evaluated along a continuum. Furthermore, he argues that we do not need a fully established abstract ideal of justice to evaluate the fairness of different institutions. He claims that we can meaningfully compare the level of justice in two institutions without positing an ideal, transcendental idea of justice. He names the opposite transcendental institutionalism.

Sen defends one of Rawls's most fundamental theoretical concepts: justice as fairness. Although this is a vague notion fraught with difficulties in any particular case, he nevertheless views it as one of Rawls's strongest insights while rejecting the necessity of Rawls's two principles of justice emerging from the original thought experiment in *A Theory of Justice*.

He credits Rawls for revitalizing the interest in the ideas of what justice means and the stress put on fairness, objectivity, equality of opportunity, removal of poverty, and freedom. However, Sen, as part of his general critique of the contractarian tradition, states that ideas about a perfectly just world do not help redress actual existing inequality. Sen faults Rawls for overemphasizing institutions as guarantors of justice and not considering the effects of human behaviour on the institutions' ability to maintain a just society. Sen believes Rawls understates the difficulty in getting everyone in society to adhere to the norms of a just society. He also claims that Rawls' position that there be only one possible outcome of the reflective equilibrium behind the veil of ignorance is misguided. In contrast to Rawls, Sen believes that multiple conflicting, yet just, principles may arise and that this undermines the multistep processes that Rawls laid out as leading to a perfectly just society (2).

Sen also draws heavily on Adam Smith and his first major work The Theory of Moral Sentiments (1759), arguing that it is Smith's most important and unduly overlooked work. One poignant criticism of the theory of the social contract is that it assumes that either the electorate or those elected to represent them will act in a manner which honours democratic principles, or, if not, will retain sufficient control to recall powers given but abused by the executive. While the tyrannical regimes of Stalin, Adolf Hitler and Mao Zedong may be viewed as 20th century aberrations, the rise of right-wing authoritarian regimes such as those in Russia, Hungary, Israel or Slovenia have or may threaten the apparent tranquillity of both interstate relations and internal cohesion. The overarching control set out in written constitutions through countering, modifying or balancing the powers of the executive with those of the judiciary and legislature may seem reassuring to the electorate, but are now frequently set aside by military regimes, as in Myanmar, by religious dictatorships, as in Iran, or by 'liberal' idealism as in Brazil or communist autocracy as in China. More worrying are the developments in the US where the Supreme Court decision (July 2024) held that the President was immune from criminal prosecution for acts conducted within the scope of his Presidency.

While Sen emphasises individual sympathy for equality rather than an institutional approach, and also embraces a wider view of what equality might comprise, there remains controversy on a number of key issues. Thus, inherited property, wealth and status, though questioned, remain contentious in establishing a level playing field and to claim that merit, through intelligence and or education, should not be rewarded more than rewards or gains afforded the less able has also attracted criticism.

While the references to commitment towards the electorate, made by Sir Kier Starmer, on his address after his appointment as Prime Minister on 7 July 2024, may not equate with any contractual obligation, it does allude to a position of trust which he asserted had been broken, implicitly, by the previous Government towards the electorate. Clearly few systems of governance permit a plebiscite enabling direct accountability for individual proposals, as envisaged by Rousseau, when the approval of specific issues may be required. At the other extreme, the transfer of absolute power to a Monarch or President, as Hobbes advocated, has transient appeal, but as with Putin, may have an allegedly democratic but thin veneer. More practical and widespread are the deployment of manifestos setting out intentions to the public before periodic elections. Most pay lip service to the concept of justice comprising fairness and equality, as argued by Rawls and Sen, but such is usually confined to citizens or denizens; the 'other' immigrants, homeless, the unemployed and the disabled rarely feature as contractual participants.

We noted how Christianity, or a belief in God and the church doctrine, albeit modified, might be absorbed within the concept of a social contract but the idea of different religions deferring to some largely secular defined ideas about governmental responsibility or indeed interfaith relations may put a strain on credibility, despite Rawls optimism, as above;

A contract, they said, would be fine
It will settle all things for all time

The Imam, the priest, the Buddhist, the Jain,
The mindful, the mad and insane
Prayed to each god for certain direction
and for the others, their needed correction
While we are all monotheists, they said
Which God is the furthest ahead?
Which prophet the best teller of truth,
Moses, Jesus, Mohammed or Ruth?
In the end, we will settle,
we'll pull the straw nettle,
the longest will win
and rejoice with a grin
(and, if mindful, an ecumenical hymn)
and the shorter, sadly, will suck it.
The contract was signed
by the sighted and blind
and carefully placed in the bin,
or possibly thrown in a bucket.

Democracy, nevertheless, for all its faults, is worth defending and the concept of the social contract worth preserving if nothing else than to remind governments that they are accountable to the electorate. As Churchill observed, democracy may be the worst system devised by man, but it is better than all the others. That sentiment allied to Rawl's view of achieving equality but qualified with Sen's broader view of what equality constitutes together with an acceptance that merit, however defined, should reflect in the scales of justice, might well constitute a Humanist approach to a social contract.

Bibliography and References

Note: many of these references and the above extracts are taken, with thanks, from the Encyclopaedia Britannica online and Wikipedia (both 2024 Editions).

Rawls, John, A Theory of Justice, Cambridge, Massachusetts: The Belknap Press of Harvard University Press, 1971, revised edition, 1999
Rawls, John, Justice and Fairness, Cambridge, Massachusetts: Belknap Press, 2001.

Samuel Freeman, (ed), Lectures on the History of Political Philosophy. Cambridge, Massachusetts: Harvard University Press, Collection of lectures, 2007

Osmani, S. R., Theory of Justice for an Imperfect World, Journal of Human Development and Capabilities. **11** (4): 599–607, 2010

Sen, Amartya, Identity and Violence; The Illusion of Destiny. Issues of our time. New York: W.W. Norton & Co., 2006

Sen, Amartya, The Idea of Justice, London: Penguin., 2010

Wikipedia, Entries on Hobbes, Locke, Rousseau, Rawls, Sen and Justice,

Encyclopaedia Britannica, Entries as above

International Encyclopaedia of Philosophy, Entries as above.

Stanford Encyclopaedia of Philosophy: Entries as above.

Animal Welfare (Animal Sentience, Cruelty, legal protection and Rights.)

What is the nature of our obligation to animals?

For most of human history, the dominant Western view has been that animals are there to do with as humans see fit (Warburton, 2021). As Grayling (2009) has observed 'Human Beings have used other animals for food and labour [and more recently] for scientific experiments without much scruple because they have standardly believed that they are not entitled to anything like the same moral consideration as Humans.'

Several religious traditions have promoted animal welfare, e.g. Buddhism and some forms of Hinduism, and some religions, such as Jainism, believe that all life should be sustained. While Descartes believed that non-human animals were automata, without soul, mind or reason, in his 'Descent of Man', Darwin (1871) believed that 'other' animals also had social, mental and moral lives to live.

In the Christian era, however, there was a biblical grant of animals to man's dominion. This contrasts with the view of many modern philosophers who believe that animals' ability to feel pain justify our consideration of their well being as of humans (Peter Singer, 2015 and Tom Regan, 1997).

Jeremy Bentham in 1789 wrote ' The question is not can they reason, nor can they talk, but can they suffer?'

This utilitarian approach was seen as a felicitous calculus by Bentham relating to the pleasure principle while John S Mill distinguished between higher and lower pleasures with the former, intellectual and moral being beyond the reach of many animals.

While Nietzsche and other philosophers have challenged the value of this approach it raises the question of animal pleasure and whether humans have an obligation to recognise and facilitate their well-being.

Are all animals to be treated equally? Are we to be like Jains and avoid killing even insects [including bedbugs, fleas and midges] or are we to follow the law of the jungle in justifying our treatment/maltreatment of other animals? If crocodiles consume the young of other crocodiles and are happy to consume human flesh, why should we be squeamish about killing them, or killing parasitic wasps, for example? Should our motive for killing be relevant? Is killing for survival, or culling for farm or environmental management, or for food or clothing, or for testing medical treatment of a different nature to killing for pleasure in a hunt?

Jack and Jill went up, until
the sky was well below them.
They fell in the sea,
well glory be,
in quite a fleeting delirium
They were swallowed alive,
By sharks who did strive
to keep the world's equilibrium.

Some have argued that provided we enable farm animals such as sheep, goats and pigs to enjoy a protected and quasi natural life, then humans have a moral obligation to kill and eat them to sustain this way of life (Zangwill, 2021) Should this practice cease, then such animals, about 5% of our meat consumption, would not be reared at all. Better to have an enjoyable, albeit short life with an abrupt end, than no life at all. Zangwill argues that historically a symbiotic relationship has evolved which benefits both man and such animals.

Three blinded mice
were eaten with parsley and rice
The contract, they said,
Was lettuce and bread
But who cares the executors cried
The details are but an aside.

Bob Percival (2023) refers to an implicit contract between the farmer and the farmed though the concept has limitations- an understanding or tolerance might be more fitting. He suggests that man historically has not been a committed herbivore; eating meat is natural but not consequentially moral?

Should we define animals as sentient and non-sentient with what consequences?

Today sentient beings are defined as animals with an ability to experience and feel sensory emotions such as pain, boredom, anxiety and pleasure. A demonstration of intelligence and possible creativity may have been apposite. It is also argued that animals should have some awareness of self to be classified as sentient. The Cambridge Declaration of Consciousness of 7 July 2012 appears to confirm this referring also to the requirement for a central nervous system. However, it is also argued that octopuses and cuttlefish are sentient where a central nervous system does not exist. The study by Duncan is informative here, 'The changing concept of animal sentience' (2006) Today rather than suggest a hierarchy of animal sentience, the debate points to a matrix or framework of considerations with different animals scoring both relatively high and low (Webster, 2006).

However, before this broader definition was accepted., the simple reference to animals recognising pain and pleasure as a litmus test of concern was qualified by the behaviourist school (James, 1904) which downplayed feelings, consciousness and awareness and focused on instinctual responses to qualify sentience.

Now, as reflected in the EU Treaty of Amsterdam 1997 which requires appropriate welfare of sentient animals, the more encompassing definition of sentience of animals is accepted.

It follows that we are now generally required to protect sentient animals from unnecessary harm. Do we have a common understanding and agreement of what is harm and what is unnecessary?

A further consideration may be that of agency as a supplement to sentience. Thus pain, for example, is not only to be felt by the animal but it is to be aware of this experience. This implies that the animal has an ability to plan life's future choices informed by past experience. For example, it has been shown that when pigs are allowed the freedom of foraging for food, rather than just being provided with it, they prefer the former and are healthier for it.

Forms of Animal Treatment and Cruelty

Is there anything wrong with using animals for food, clothing, entertainment and research provided treatment minimises 'unnecessary' pain and suffering?

Animal rights theorists argue that most use of animals is unjustified and a cause of suffering; they should not be treated as property. Issues include.

a) Intensive agricultural farming
Chicken batteries; veal crates; pig gestation crates; salmon farms; Beef and other cattle and sheep rearing and slaughter.

b) Treatment such as branding, castration, de-horning, ear tagging, tail docking and nose ringing, amongst others may be considered 'inhumane' and cruel.

c) Fur industry.

d) Zoo-sadism linked to psychological disorders.

e) Filming and animal maltreatment, e.g. 'Heavens Gate'.

f) The use of trip wires against horses as in Rambo 3, and 'The 13th Warrior'.

g) YouTube hosts thousands of examples of animal cruelty.

h) Circuses

i) Animal fighting-cocks, bulls, rattlesnake, rodeos or round-ups provide further examples.

Forms of maltreatment may be either active or passive, the latter largely focused on neglect.

However, some human use of animals may be seen as beneficial or even symbiotic.

1. Working animals in military; bomb disposal, use of dolphins, horses and dogs in particular
2. Sheep dogs in working farm.
3. Dogs for the blind
4. Animals as pets
5. Horse riding and racing
6. Rearing, endangered animals in a secure but restricted environment
7. Pasture Farming?

International and Regional Laws and Obligations

The history of international and national provision to protect and promote animal welfare has shown progressive intent to broaden the scope of application. Thus: -

The World Organisation for Animal Health [OIE] has now identified and promoted five freedoms for animals.

1] Freedom from hunger or thirst
2] Freedom from discomfort
3] Freedom from pain, injury of disease
4] Freedom to express normal behaviour
5] Freedom from fear and distress

There is no international treaty on animal welfare but the *Universal Declaration of Animal Rights*, as of 2014 had support of 46 countries and the RSPCA.

European Conventions

A number of conventions are designed to protect animal welfare; thus the 1976 and 1992 Conventions on farming, the 1979 Convention on slaughter, the 1987 Convention on pet animals, the 2003 Convention on transport and the 1986 and 1996 Conventions on animal vertebrates and science testing. These are designed to set standards of acceptable treatment to be followed by the member European countries.

European Union

Similarly, the 1997 Treaty of Amsterdam and the 2007 Treaty of Lisbon require those responsible to pay full regard to animal welfare while recognising religious, regional and cultural differences. Clearly there is some difference of view and dubiety about inclusion and acceptance of practices in this regard.

EU Directives

There are also EU directives on transport and slaughter as well as farming practices relating, inter alia, to pigs, calves and broilers.

EU directives relate to animal experiments, cosmetics, pets, fur [seal pups, cats and dogs] fishing and crustaceans, zoos and wild animals.

Will the bonfire of EU regulations promised by Rees-Mogg before the 2024 elections and change of Government, include all or some of these? Not yet: but there is apprehension that animal welfare may be compromised by the motive for profit and to counteract the adverse impact on the economy created by Brexit. Access to the US market in chickens, for example, may tempt a lowering of standards not only affecting food consumption but also animal welfare.

UK and Scottish Laws

Animal Health and Welfare Act 2006

In contradistinction to the above concerns, this UK wide Act provides measures to promote welfare. The Act brings together and updates legislation that exists to promote the welfare of vertebrate animals, other than man and those in the wild. The categories of animals that are protected under the Act depend on the offence in question. For example, the duty to ensure an animal's welfare only applies to animals that are owned or for which someone is otherwise responsible, but the cruelty and fighting offences have a wider application. The Act has only limited application to animals in research establishments, the welfare of which is regulated by the Animals (Scientific Procedures) Act 1986. The Act aligns welfare standards for farmed animals, which have generally kept in line with developments in scientific understanding, and non-farmed animals which are largely protected by laws formulated in the early twentieth century.

Moreover, *The Animal Health and Welfare (Scotland Act) 2006*, as amended, principally by the *Animal Health and Welfare (Scotland) Act 2020* under devolved powers, provides for a duty of care on pet owners and others responsible to ensure welfare needs are met. It states

a) Guidance and penalties
b) Farm animal welfare, setting out standards in guidance and regulations under Animal and Plant Welfare Agency [APHA]; guidance relates to chickens, cattle, pigs and sheep and others. includes disease control and powers of inspection and
c) Establishing the Highlands Veterinary Service Scheme
d) Horse welfare and other Equidae
e) Pet Animal Welfare
f) Standards for Slaughter and Transport
g) Standards for Circuses and performing animals.
h) Standards for Zoos and dangerous wild animals.

The 2020 Act relates to protection, powers and penalties.
In amending various animal welfare and wildlife crime legislation, this Act aims to increase penalties for sentient animal welfare and health offences. It will also increase penalties for wildlife crime. Thus it

- introduces fixed penalties animal welfare and health offences
- holds anyone accountable who deliberately causes harm to a sentient animal
- increases fines and/or custodial sentences in relation to certain wildlife offences

Inspectors and constables will be able to act on animal welfare issues. An offence does not need to have taken place. They will not need to wait for a court order. This will allow them to ease the suffering of animals. This means they can:

- administer treatment to sick or injured animals
- transfer to animal welfare facilities.
- euthanise animals
- re-home animals

Further information is found in the Explanatory Notes to the Act.

Animal [Sentience] Act 2022.

This Act was informed by a study undertaken by the LSE and sponsored by the Government to advise on measures which should be considered and possibly adopted for sentient animals.

a) The Act applies to all of UK.
b) An Animal Sentience Committee is established.
c) It reports to relevant Governments on sentient animals affected by Gov. policy.
d) Sentient animal are vertebrates, cephalopods and decapod crustaceans i.e. octopuses, cuttlefish and lobsters; these may be added to by regulations.
e) Reports must be responded to by governments.
f) In effect the Act recognises that animals other than humans are feeling beings able to experience pain, fear and enjoyment.

Fox and other mammal Hunting

In Scotland, the *Protection of Wild Mammals (Scotland) Act 2002* restricted pack hunting and required the fox to be shot. The Hunting with Dogs Bill, now before the Scottish Parliament, limits hunting to two dogs but permits greater numbers to be used under licence. The Countryside Alliance argues for automatic permission for pack hunting while the Green Party argues that the licencing provision is too permissive.

Animal Rights

While we have touched on some aspects of animal rights these have largely focussed on human treatment and the avoidance of suffering, but what are positive rights?

Animal rights are often considered to be moral principles grounded in the belief that animals deserve the ability to live as they wish, without being subject to the desires of human beings. This includes a right to life, liberty and freedom from suffering and possibly to live a life which permits a realisation of 'natural' behaviour.

Animals should not be viewed as property or used for human benefit. The argument for such rights, particularly for mammals is

They have similar levels of biological complexity as humans.

They are conscious and are aware of their own existence.

They may make conscious decisions about how they live to optimise their conditions.

The quality and length of life matters to them.

Arguments against animal rights include.

They act on instinct and not on rational thought (Thomas Aquinas))

They don't behave morally.

They are here to serve humans (Biblical interpretation)) and don't have souls.

Rights are restricted to a moral community i.e. humans.

If animals cannot articulate their rights, why should they have any?

If animals don't have/respect rights towards each other, why should humans invent their rights by protecting them from each other as well as from human predation? (M. Warnock, 'An Intelligent Person's Guide to Ethics', 1998)

If animals have no duties or obligations to Humans, why should humans have such towards animals.

Humanist Perspective

The Amsterdam Declaration as amended in 2022, provides

a) A free person has duties to others...and beyond this to all sentient beings
b) We recognise that we are part of nature and accept responsibility for the impact we have on humans and the rest of the natural world.

Is this anthropocentric, biocentric or speciesism?

Clearly, this assertion of duties and responsibilities begs a number of critical questions. Do we owe a duty to permit or promote the realisation of instinctive behaviour in our pets? Should we allow our cats to roam and to catch birds and mice; and if so, have we behaved appropriately to such predated animals? Are we to treat non-sentient species, or rather those we assume to be non-sentient, with like consideration to sentient species. Are bed bugs and mosquitoes deserving of like consideration to elephants and bats? Should we treat gorillas and monkeys with greater consideration than crocodiles and snakes? Is our desire to consume meat an atavistic deviation and an expression of speciesism as well as unjustified anthropocentrism? Is our cultivation of animal and fish farms for food warranted, given the option of eating vegetables?

The Humanist Declarations do not answer these questions directly; but they do assert firstly that we should recognise both laws and conventions which promote animal well-being and secondly that we should avoid cruelty to animals and allow sentient animals some fulfilment in their existence, even if our anthropocentric need for food and sustenance results in such existence being relatively short and designed to meet our needs. It is also apparent that the humanist view of duties and responsibilities is not static. It will alter in accordance not only with scientific development and discovery but also with changing social conditions and attitudes. Singer argues not that we should treat all animals equally but that we give them equal consideration. While that may sound a defensible approach, it may also prove unrealistic. Our moral integrity is unlikely to be put in peril when we swat a fly or mosquito or crush a louse or bedbug. Consequently, an element of relativism and speciesism may well remain an accepted failing in the Humanist position but rational alternatives are equally hard to find. What of a biocentric approach which ascribes equal value to all species? Again, a sense of pragmatic realism would allow the Humanist, if not all humanity, to play centre stage not only in meeting his or her needs but also in acknowledging that we are the species best placed to play a positive role in the protection and promotion of others, however limited such roles my prove to be. Pragmatic realism sounds better than common sense and we know that such is seldom common and often irrational. Lord Denning referred to the wisdom of the man on the Clapham omnibus, or clapped-out omnibus in today's parlance, perhaps.

Contemporary Developments

Does climate change impact on human obligations towards sentient and other animals?

Many more species are now threatened with impoverished habitats and even extinction, polar bears being an example. Increased hurricanes, landslides, droughts, fires and periods of intensive heat and cold may have very damaging impacts on mammals and insects and flora.

Human expansion and population increase has affected animal habitats adversely. For example, African and Indian elephants and reindeer from the Arctic Circle have their normal migrations disrupted and terminated.

It is now worth considering the Human impact at a worldwide level. According to a recent study (Ron Milo, 2024), while the total biomass of the human race accounts for only 0.01 of the world's biomass, plants account for 82% and bacteria 13%. The transformation of the planet by human activity has created a new era, the Anthropocene. Poultry farming makes up 70% of all birds on the planet, just 30% being wild. 60% of the earth's mammals are livestock, mostly cattle and pigs, humans account for 36% with only about 4% being wild. About half the world's animals are thought to have been lost in the last 50 years and only 20% of the marine mammals remain. In comparison with the biomass of man, there are three times more, viruses, three times more worms, 12 times more fish and 17 times more insects, spiders and crustaceans (Guardian, 2018).

Human use of plastics has affected the ocean habitats, and the use of pesticides and intensive agricultural and fish farming are continuing threats to many species. The responsibility of the humanist, it would seem, is to respond positively to such developments and to adjust individual and social behaviour to protect and enhance the prospect of survival and the living conditions threatened by these and like changes. Moreover, it is clear that many of our current activities, such as fishing from the ocean beds and the building of wind turbines, may impact adversely on wildlife and its habitat. The duty is to minimise such impact.

Plants, Fungi and other living things.

Given the increasing awareness of the complexity of non-animal life [the interconnectedness of trees and fungi for example,] there may be a case for not only communicating with this form of life as potentially sentient but also considering action to minimise harm, if not pain? and to promote well-being not only from an anthropocentric perspective of self-interest. But perhaps we should await the day of the triffids?

References

Wikipedia, Cruelty to Animals, Animal Welfare and Rights, 2024
The Silence of Animals, John Grey, Penguin Philosophy, 2014

Justin Gregg, If Nietzsche were a Narwhal, Hodder and Stoughton, 2023

Peter Godfrey-Smith, Other Minds, William Collins Books, 2017

Peter Singer, Animal Liberation, 2015 and 2023

Julian Franklin, Animal Rights and Moral Philosophy, University of Columbia Press,2006

Netflix 'My teacher Octopus', Erlich and Reed, 2020

BBC World Service, 'What do you think you are? available as podcasts. 10 and 17 January 2023

Regan, T.,' The Case for Animal Rights' Routledge and Kegan, London, 1983

PETA, Guide on animal welfare

Nick Zangwill, 'Our Moral Duty to Eat Meat', Cambridge University Press 14/6/2021

M. Warnock, 'An Intelligent Person's Guide to Ethics', 1998   Ian Duncan, Ian 'The changing concept of animal sentience', Applied   Animal behaviour Science, 2006

John Webster, 'Sentience in Animals' Vol 100, Issues 1-2, Oct. 2006

Bob Percival, 'The Meat Paradox' BBC podcast Radio 4, 30 Jan, 1 to 3 Feb. 2023

Martha Nussbaum, 'Justice for Animals', Simon and Schuster, 2023.

Lorna Findlayson, 'Let them eat Oysters', LRB August 2023

A C Grayling, 'Ideas that Matter', Phoenix Books, 2008

Nigel Warburton, Everyday Philosophy; the worrying link over cruelty to animals. The New European, Nov. 2021

Charles Darwin, Descent of Man, 1871

Ryan Haliday, Ed, Daily Stoic, Podcast

Ron Milo, Prof., Proceedings of the National Academy of Sciences, May 2018

Damien Carrington, Humans have destroyed 83%of wildlife, Guardian Newspaper, 21, May 20

Climate Change and Global Warming

The Problem

One of the persistent ironies about our changing climate is that while the world, excepting the lunatic fringe of deniers, is well aware of the problem, its extent and, also, critically what to do about it, yet those various targets set to counterbalance the impact of global warming are regularly failed to be met.

One reason is the inevitable concern of successive democratic governments to accede to the demands for short term survival and re-election by appeasing the various interests of the electorate and the energy extractors, generators and suppliers in sustaining the existing modes of power and its transmission. Another is the apparent cost of effecting a radical change to wind, solar, tidal and nuclear power supply and the means of reducing power consumption, particularly by insulation, private transport regulation and public transport provision. In addition. the global human population is expanding and the demand for energy for home, transport, holidays and industry is also increasing.

The current rise in global average temperature has arisen from burning fossil fuels since the Industrial Revolution. Deforestation and some agricultural and industrial practices add to greenhouse gases which absorb some of the heat that the Earth receives from sunlight and the lower atmosphere. Carbon dioxide, the primary greenhouse gas driving global warming, has grown by about 50% and is at levels unseen for millions of years. A further obstacle to change is the very significant political, social and financial weight exercised by large international companies and conglomerates with a vested interest in minimizing the impact on income growth by effecting rapid and substantial change.

Climate change has an increasingly large impact. Deserts expand, heat waves and wild fires, as now seen in Canada and around Athens are becoming increasingly common. Arctic warming has contributed to thawing permafrost, glacial retreat, and a decline in sea ice, [see Wikipedia, Climate Change]. Higher temperatures are also causing weather extremes such as severe droughts and storms causing significant loss of life and property. Many species are forced to relocate and even become extinct through rapid environmental change in coral reefs, pastures, mountains as well as the Arctic and Antarctic. Even if efforts to minimize future warming are successful, some effects will continue for centuries. The effects of these include sea level rise and acidification of the seas with extensive algae growth in addition to pollution from other sources, such as plastics.

The World Health Organisation (WHO) identifies climate change as one of the biggest threats to global health in the 21st century. It states that societies and ecosystems will experience more severe risks without action to limit warming although adapting to change through measures such as flood control and deploying drought and water tolerant planting may reduce risks. While poorer communities are responsible for a small contribution to change in the climate yet have the least ability to adapt and are the most vulnerable.

Climate change is impacting human lives and health in a variety of ways. It threatens the essential ingredients of good health – clean air, safe drinking water, nutritious food supply and safe shelter – and has the potential to undermine decades of progress in global health.

Between 2030 and 2050, climate change is expected to cause approximately 250,000 additional deaths per year from malnutrition, malaria, diarrhoea and heat stress alone. The direct damage costs to health are estimated to be between US$ 2–4 billion per year by 2030. Areas with weak health infrastructure – mostly in developing countries – will be the least able to cope without assistance to prepare and respond.

Greenhouse gas emissions that result from the extraction and burning of fossil fuels are major contributors to both climate change and air pollution. Many policies and individual measures, WHO claim, such as transport, food and energy use choices, have the potential to reduce greenhouse gas emissions and produce major health co-benefits, particularly by abating air pollution. The phase-out of polluting energy systems, for example, or the promotion of public transportation and active movement, could both lower carbon emissions and cut the burden of household and ambient air pollution, which cause 7 million premature deaths per year. Many climate change impacts have been felt in recent years, with 2023 the warmest on record at +1.48°C (2.66°F) since regular tracking began in 1850 Additional warming will increase these impacts and can trigger tipping points such as melting all of the Greenland ice sheet.

The countries which pollute the most are China with 30%, USA with 15% followed by India 7%, Russia 5% and Japan 4%.

What to do?

Under the 2015 Paris Agreement, nations collectively agreed to keep warming "well under 2°C". However, with pledges made under the Agreement, global warming would still reach about 2.7°C (4.9°F) by the end of the century.

Limiting warming to 1.5°C would require halving emissions by 2030 and achieving net-zero emissions by 2050.

Climate change can be mitigated by reducing the rate at which greenhouse gases are emitted into the atmosphere, and by increasing the rate at which carbon dioxide is removed from the atmosphere. This requires far-reaching, systemic changes on an unprecedented scale in energy, land, cities, transport, buildings, and industry.

The UN Environmental program estimates that countries need to honour their commitments in the Paris Agreement within the next decade to limit global warming to 2°C. An even greater level of reduction is required to meet the 1.5°C goal, with pledges made under the Paris Agreement as of October 2021, global warming would still have a 66% chance of reaching about 2.7°C (range: 2.2–3.2°C) by the end of the century. Globally, limiting warming to 2°C may result in higher economic benefits than economic costs.

While there is no single approach to limit global warming to 1.5 or 2°C, most plans envisage a major increase in the use of renewable energy in combination with increased energy efficiency measures to generate the needed greenhouse gas reductions. Changes would also be necessary in agriculture and forestry, such as preventing deforestation and restoring natural ecosystems by reforestation.

Other approaches to mitigating climate change have a higher level of risk. Scenarios that limit global warming to 1.5°C typically project the large-scale use of carbon dioxide removals over the 21st century. There are concerns, though, about over-reliance on the technologies employed, and the environmental impacts. Solar Radiation Modification (SRM) is also a possible supplement to deep reductions in emissions. However, SRM raises significant ethical and legal concerns, and the risks are not adequately understood.

Clean energy

Coal, oil, and natural gas remain the primary global energy sources even as renewables are increasing rapidly. Renewable energy is key to limiting climate change. For decades, fossil fuels have accounted for roughly 80% of the world's energy use. The remaining share has been split between nuclear power and renewables. Fossil fuel use is expected to peak in absolute terms prior to 2030 and then to decline, with coal use experiencing the sharpest reductions. Renewables represented 75% of all new electricity generation installed in 2019, nearly all solar and wind. Other forms of clean energy, such as nuclear and hydropower, currently have a significant share of the energy supply. However, their future growth forecasts appear limited in comparison.

In Scotland the new hydropower proposed for Coire has had initial approval. Once complete, Coire Glas would be capable of delivering 30GW of long duration storage. The scheme would take excess energy from the grid and use it to pump water 500 meters up a hill from Loch Lochy to a vast upper reservoir equivalent to nearly 11,000 Olympic-sized swimming pools where it would be stored before being released to power the grid when wind output is low and customer demand is high. Coire Glas would begin generating enough renewable energy to be able to power three million homes in just under five minutes. Critically, the Coire Glas project could provide this level of firm, flexible power for up to 24 hours non-stop. The UK Government's decision on how it intends to financially support the deployment of long-duration electricity storage, as set out in the British Energy Security Strategy remains unclear. This could include the introduction of a 'revenue stabilisation mechanism' in the form of an adapted Cap and Floor scheme to support investment in long-duration storage. This would also be alongside broader consideration of how the electricity market, including the Capacity Mechanism and the Flexibility Markets, value the contribution of low carbon flexible assets such as pumped storage. Coire Glas is expected to be one of the biggest engineering projects in the Scottish Highlands since the 1943 Hydro Electric Development (Scotland) Act kickstarted the construction of major hydro-electric schemes across Scotland 80 years ago.

Electricity generated from renewable sources would also need to become the main energy source for heating and transport. Transport will transfer from internal combustion and towards electric, public transit, and active transport such as cycling and walking. For shipping and flying, low-carbon fuels would reduce emissions. Heating could be increasingly de-carbonised with technologies like heat pumps for which the Scottish Government extended grants for up to £9k per household in 2024.

There are obstacles to the continued rapid growth of clean energy, including renewables. For wind and solar, there are environmental and land use concerns for new projects. Wind and solar produce energy intermittently with seasonal variability. Battery storage may be expanded, energy provision and demand can be matched, and long-distance transmission can smooth variability of renewable outputs. In August 2024, Government announced a intention to extend the power network through installations of underwater links between Peterhead and Drax. This £3.4 billion funding package has been awarded to build a proposed new subsea and underground 500 km cable which could power up to 2 million homes. Eastern Green Link 2 (EGL2) is the first of 26 projects to complete a fast-track process to secure funding through Ofgem's new ASTI framework. ASTI accelerates the funding process by up to two years, allowing electricity generated by offshore wind to be delivered to British consumers sooner. However, while such proposals upgrade the National Grid and enable the transfer of Scottish generated power to England and Wales are clearly welcome, the failure to provide underwater links to enable power generated in the Hebrides, Orkney and Shetland to be efficiently transmitted to the mainland is regretted.

In November 2020, The UK Government under Boris Johnston issued a White Paper, 'The Ten Point Plan for a Green Industrial Revolution', with the ten points as follow: -

1.Advancing Offshore Wind, 2. Driving the Growth of Low Carbon Hydrogen, 3. Delivering New and Advanced Nuclear Power, 4. Accelerating the Shift to Zero Emission Vehicles, 5. Green Public Transport, Cycling and Walking 6, Jet Zero and Green Ships,7. Greener Buildings, 8. Investing in Carbon Capture, Usage and Storage, 9. Protecting Our Natural Environment, 10. Green Finance and Innovation.

The plan involved, inter alia, the allocation of £385m for nuclear research and development with Rolls Royce allocated £215 for small modular reactors. A number of countries, including, Canada, Japan, Czech and UK are exploring different technologies for both Small Nuclear Reactors (SNR) and Micro Nuclear Reactors (MNR) with expected power outputs of a tenth of the larger nuclear reactors while SNR output is about a third. The SNRs may be appropriate for less accessible areas while the MNRs are seen as having a variety of uses. Both systems may benefit from local assembly of components and in the case of MNRs they may be self-regulating and need less active monitoring. The IAEA (the International Atomic Energy Agency) plays a key role in supporting and coordinating the development of SMRs

Bio-energy is often not carbon-neutral and may have negative consequences for food security. The growth of nuclear power is constrained by controversy around location, radioactive waste and accidents in particular. Hydropower growth is limited by the fact that the best sites have been developed, and new projects are confronting increased social and environmental concerns. While solar power is less problematic, the siting and displacement of agriculture remain significant issues. One proposal to ease the last, is to construct solar panels on the extensive roofs of industrial, commercial and agricultural buildings.

However, such 'clean energy' improves human health by minimizing climate change as well as reducing air pollution deaths which were estimated at 7 million annually in 2016. Meeting the Paris Agreement goals that limit warming to a 2°C increase could save about a million of those lives per year by 2050, whereas limiting global warming to 1.5°C could save further lives and simultaneously increase energy security and reduce poverty. Improving air quality also has economic benefits which may be larger than mitigation costs.

Climate justice

Policy designed to promote social justice (Climate Justice) tries to address human rights issues and social inequality. According to proponents of climate justice, the costs of climate adaptation should be paid by those most responsible for climate change, while the beneficiaries of payments should be those suffering impacts. One way this can be addressed in practice is to have wealthy nations pay poorer countries to adapt.

Oxfam found that in 2023 the wealthiest 10% of people were responsible for 50% of global emissions, while the bottom 50% were responsible for just 8%. Production of emissions is another way to look at responsibility: under that approach, the top 21 fossil fuel companies would owe cumulative climate reparations of $5.4 trillion over the period 2025–2050. To achieve a just transmission, people working in the fossil fuel sector would also need other jobs, and their communities would need investments.

International climate agreements

UNFCCC

Nearly all countries in the world are parties to the 1994 UN Framework Convention (UNFCCC). The goal of the UNFCCC is to prevent dangerous human interference with the climate system. As stated in the convention, this requires that greenhouse gas concentrations are stabilised in the atmosphere at a level where ecosystems can adapt naturally to climate change, food production is not threatened, and economic development can be sustained. The UNFCCC does not itself restrict emissions but rather provides a framework for protocols that do. Global emissions have risen since the UNFCCC was signed. Its yearly conferences are the stage of global negotiations.

The 1997 Kyoto Protocol extended the UNFCCC and included legally binding commitments for most developed countries to limit their emissions. During the negotiations, the G77 (representing developing countries) pushed for a mandate requiring them to take "the lead" in reducing their emissions, since developed countries contributed most to the accumulation of greenhouse gases in the atmosphere. Per-capita emissions were also still relatively low in developing countries and developing countries would need to emit more to meet their development needs.

The 2009 Copenhagen Accord has been widely portrayed as disappointing because of its low goals, and was rejected by poorer nations including the G77. Associated parties aimed to limit the global temperature rise to below 2°C. The Accord set the goal of sending $100 billion per year to developing countries for mitigation and adaptation by 2020, and proposed the founding of the Green Climate Fund. As of 2020, only $ 83.3 billion had been delivered. Only by 2023 was the target expected to be achieved.

In 2015 all UN countries negotiated the Paris Agreement which aims to keep global warming well below 2.0°C and contains an aspirational goal of keeping warming under 1.5°C. The agreement replaced the Kyoto Protocol. Unlike Kyoto, no binding emission targets were set in the Paris Agreement. Instead, a set of procedures was made binding. Countries have to regularly set ever more ambitious goals and reevaluate these goals every five years. The Paris Agreement restated that developing countries must be financially supported. As of October 2021, 194 states and the EU have signed the treaty and 191 states and the EU have ratified or acceded to the agreement.

Collectively, the three post-2015 agendas for action building on the existing UN framework (the UNFCCC, as noted above) are the Paris Agreement, the 2030 Agenda for Sustainable Development and the Sendai Framework for Disaster Risk Reduction - provide the foundation for sustainable, low-carbon and resilient development under a changing climate.

Achieving the primary goal of the Paris Agreement - to keep the average global temperature rise well below 2C degrees and as close as possible to 1.5C above pre-industrial levels - is vital to the achievement of all three Agendas. The global average temperature has already increased by around one degree, since then underlining the urgency of action if we are to stay as close as possible to 1.5C degrees.

A co-operative and coherent way in pursuing climate action and sustainable development offers the strongest approach to enable countries and relevant agencies to achieve their objectives efficiently and quickly under the Paris Agreement and the 2030 Agenda for Sustainable Development Goals (SDGs). The 2030 Agenda encompasses 17 SDGs, 169 targets and a declaration text articulating the principles of integration, universality, transformation and a global partnership. The agenda came into being through a unique global process of an open working group, which jointly developed the 17 SDGs that were subsequently agreed on by all UN member states. The SDGs include the social, environmental and economic dimensions of development. They aim to provide a social foundation while ensuring that human development takes place within earth's biophysical boundaries. At national levels, implementation of the 2030 Agenda varies from country to country, and is based on national needs and ambitions but subject to governmental priorities, commitment and resources. At the international level, the High-Level Political Forum (HLPF) meets annually under the auspices of the UN Economic and Social Council (ECOSOC) to discuss Voluntary National Reviews (VNRs) as part of the official follow-up and review mechanism of the 2030 Agenda. However, individual countries are left to set up institutional processes for implementing the SDGs at national and subnational levels through National Sustainable Development Strategies (NSDS's). Countries can also work in partnership with other countries to learn from each other's experiences on challenges in implementation (see 'Connections between the Paris Agreement and the 2030 Agenda', Stockholm Environmental Institute, Working Paper 2023).

Ironically, the 1987 Montreal Protocol to stop emitting ozone-depleting gases, may have been more effective at curbing greenhouse gas emissions than the Kyoto Protocol specifically designed to do so. A 2016 amendment (Kigali) to the Montreal Protocol aims to reduce the emissions of hydrofluorocarbons, a group of powerful greenhouse gases which served as a replacement for banned ozone-depleting gases. This made the Montreal Protocol a stronger agreement against climate change.

National responses

In 2019, the UK became the first national government to declare a climate emergency. Other countries then followed suit. That same year, the EU Parliament declared a "climate and environmental emergency". The EU Commission presented its European Green Deal with the goal of making the EU carbon-neutral by 2050. In 2021, the European Commission released its "Fit for 35" legislation package, which contains guidelines for the car industry; all new cars on the European market must be zero emission from 2035. As noted above the UK 10 Point plan is a response to both the emergency declared and the Paris Agreement. The United Kingdom's Ten Point Plan is very similar to its Environmental Act of 2021 but the two plans are slightly different. Both plans strive to protect nature and biodiversity but ultimately – the U.K. Environment Act of 2021 is more concerned with helping local governments implement regulations that will improve the overall well-being of the environment: such as mitigating waste, recycling, air and water quality, and preserving nature through the likes of the Greenbelt.

Major countries in Asia have made similar pledges to implement the Paris Agreement: South Korea and Japan have committed to become carbon-neutral by 2050, and China by 2060. While India has strong incentives for renewables, it also plans a significant expansion of coal in the country. Vietnam is among very few coal-dependent, fast-developing countries that pledged to phase out unabated coal power by the 2040s or as soon as possible thereafter.

As of 2021, based on information from 48 national climate plans, which then represent 40% of the parties to the Paris Agreement, estimated total greenhouse gas emissions will be 0.5% lower compared to 2010 levels, well below the 45% or 25% reduction goals to limit global warming to 1.5°C or 2°C, respectively. Climate change in Scotland is causing a range of impacts, and its mitigation and adaptation is a matter for the devolved Scottish Parliament. It has already changed the timings of spring events such as leaf unfolding, bird migration and egg-laying. Severe effects are likely to occur on biodiversity.

Greenhouse gas emissions

Scotland's greenhouse gas emissions only accounted for 10% of the UK's emissions in 2003, when figures were published. 37% of Scottish emissions are in energy supply and 17% in transport. Between 1990 and 2007, Scottish net emissions have reduced by 18.7%. The industrial processes sector had the largest decrease, of 72% with a reduction of 48% in the public sector trailing closely behind.

Temperature and weather changes

In Scotland, the effects of climate change can be seen in raised atmospheric temperature, seasonal changes, increased rainfall and less snow cover. These changes have a significant impact on the growing, breeding and migration seasons, as well as species abundance and diversity.

Climate Change (Emissions Reduction Targets) (Scotland) Act 2019

This Act amends the Climate Change (Scotland) Act 2009 to make provision setting targets for the reduction of greenhouse gases emissions and to make provision about advice, plans and reports in relation to those targets, with the objective of Scotland contributing appropriately to the world's efforts to deliver on the Paris Agreement 2015. It establishes a Citizen's Assembly as a consultative body on reference from Parliament.

The Scottish Government issued a White Paper in 2019 'UK energy policy and Scotland's contribution to security of supply'; this is the summary of conclusions. ◻ The first duty of government on energy policy is to guarantee security of supply for domestic consumers and businesses by maintaining a sufficient reserve capacity – yet, the UK government is failing in that regard. ◻ We are facing the highest black-out risk in a generation, with reserve energy margins falling to as low as 2 per cent in the very near future. ◻ The consequences of this are grave with upward pressure on consumer bills, extra costs for business and a deterrent effect on inward investment. ◻ UK Government's own energy White Paper (2011) said low-capacity margins could trigger supply shortages costing the UK economy up to £600 million. ◻ Short-term measures to plug the energy gap all entail additional expense for consumers – for example, payments to persuade energy-intensive users to consume less energy or payments to generators to bring back retired plant ◻ Repeated failures of Westminster governments to take necessary decisions and apply policy consistently have worsened the outlook – Electricity Market Reform has been mishandled leading to a withdrawal of investment in new capacity at a time when it is urgently required to keep the lights on. ◻ Due to high levels of investor uncertainty existing capacity is being mothballed, investment in new capacity delayed or withdrawn completely – so new capacity is coming onto the grid at a rate slower than expected. ◻ The recent Budget decision to slow the deployment of energy efficiency measures will make a difficult situation even worse. ◻Scotland is a substantial and reliable net exporter of electricity, with over a quarter of all Scottish generation exported in 2012 – effectively, Scotland is now the UK's energy reserve. ◻ The most cost-effective location in these islands for renewable energy generation is Scotland – Scotland is producing clean power in record amounts and consistently supplying over a third of all the UK's clean energy. ◻ Energy investments in Scotland are helping to keep the lights on across these islands and Scotland's renewable generation is necessary to meet the UK Government's legally binding climate change and renewables targets.

While this outburst appears to be both a boast and a moan, it does underline both the critical position of Scotland regarding energy supply to the UK and the sense of injustice regarding the lack of coordinated planning and investment by the UK Government.

Transport

Greenhouse gas emissions from Road transport makes up around $1/5^{th}$ of the UK total; only 0.5% of licensed vehicles were ultra-low by 2018 while the number of total vehicles had increased by 6% between 1990 and 2017, while vehicle miles increased by almost 30% over a like period. The UK government's road to Zero strategy includes the ambition that by 2050 'almost' every car and van will be zero emission. The Committee on Climate Change (CCC)'s net zero report notes that to achieve this, non-compliant vehicle sales will have to end in all likelihood by 2035. Low Carbon Emission Zones (LEZ), bike lanes, public transport subsidies and integration rail, bus and train in particular all need to be addressed more effectively.

The UK Department for Energy, Security and Net Zero provides a chart comparing the emissions per passenger kilometre arising from different modes of transport, This chart demonstrates that Domestic flights followed by diesel and electric cars then short and long haul flights leave the greatest carbon footprint while amongst the least are rail, tram, underground, coach (longer travel) and ferries by foot passenger.

It noted that using a bike or walking for short trips would reduce travel emissions by about 75%. For medium length trips using a train instead of a car would reduce emissions by 80%, and by 86% as an alternative to domestic flights.

With reference to air transport, the lack of fuel duty places this form of transport in a favoured position regarding competition but this results inevitably in its position as one of the worst, if not the worst, in respect of carbon emissions. 1.9% of global carbon emissions come from aviation, from passenger travel and freight, as well as domestic and international aviation. 81% of aviation emissions come from passenger travel, and 19% from freight. From passenger aviation, 60% of emissions come from international travel, and 40% from domestic.

Work has been done, in particular, to make more efficient engines and to explore alternative fuels but the great dependence of this form of transport for holidays and work inhibits a more robust approach to change. Governments, during Covid lockdown were shown the possibilities of restricted air travel including the potential for staycation, stay at home holidays, but the manifest public desire for travel for the better off re-enforced the popularity of air flight and the danger presented to governments in imposing unpopular restrictions. Moreover, the global population increase and the percentage increase in those seeking a holiday abroad points to an inevitable increase in carbon emissions without much greater measures of control.

It might be thought that alternative holidays by cruising might lessen the carbon footprint; but the facts demonstrate otherwise. Take for example the environmental impact of cruise ships.

Cruise ships are often likened to floating cities because of their size and capacity. For example, the Icon of the Seas can accommodate over 9,000 passengers and crew members. This ship alone would release around 15 million tons of CO_2 annually, equivalent to 2.2 million cars.

Furthermore, on average, cruise ships and other maritime vessels, such as cargo ships, tankers, oil tankers, and ferries, account for about 3% of greenhouse gas emissions yearly. On average, a cruise ship emits 250g of CO_2 per passenger kilometre travelled—much more carbon intensity than a short hall flight.

One area of concern for cruise ships like the Icon of the Seas is methane emissions or what is known as "methane slip ", referring to leakage during combustion from pressure dual-fuel engines.

They have been criticised for their harmful effects on the oceans, including the dumping of sewage and wastewater, emissions of air pollutants and greenhouse gases, and the use of heavy fuel oil. To put this into perspective, a medium-sized cruise ship can emit as much particulate matter as one million cars.

A week-long cruise can be more carbon-intensive than a similar duration stay in a hotel combined with air travel. The continuous operation of cruise ships, even when docked, leads to constant fuel burn and emissions. In contrast, the carbon footprint of a flight is confined to the travel duration, and modern hotels increasingly adopt green practices, like energy-efficient lighting and renewable energy sources.

However, this comparison varies significantly depending on the distance of the flight, type of aircraft, the efficiency of the cruise ship, and the sustainability practices of the hotels involved. Generally, air travel emits more CO_2 per passenger kilometre than sea travel, but cruises extend over longer periods, often tipping the balance.

In January, the world's largest cruise ship set sail on its seven-day maiden voyage from the Port of Miami (BBC report, 2024). The vessel, named Icon of the Seas, cost Royal Caribbean $2bn (£1.6bn) to build, has 18 decks, seven swimming pools and more than 40 restaurants, bars and lounges. It is 365m (1,195ft) long – five times as large as the Titanic.

The ship is powered by liquified natural gas (LNG) which Royal Caribbean has described as "the cleanest fuel available." But environmental campaigners say it worsens the situation because it leaks polluting methane into the atmosphere, which is about 80 times worse than carbon dioxide (CO_2) over a 20-year time span.

The industry's impact on the natural world is only set to grow as cruising booms. Ticket sales for cruise ships in 2024 are higher than ever. By the end of the year, 360 cruise ships are projected to have carried a total of 30m passengers, a 9.2% increase compared to 2019, before Covid-19 hit.

We have noted that even the most efficient cruise ships may pollute more than flying, according to analysis by the International Council on Clean Transportation (ICCT), a US-based non-profit organisation.

Waste is another major problem. More than 8.5 billion gallons of toxic waste were discharged off the west coast of Canada by cruise ships travelling to and from Alaska in 2019.

Plus, noise pollution from ships harms marine life. A 2012 study found that mid-range noise from ships sonar overlaps with blue whales calls to each other, forcing them to repeat their vocalisations and disrupting their communication.

Cleaning up cruising

Port cities are starting to crack down on cruise ships amid mounting health and environmental concerns. In 2021, Venice banned cruise ships from entering its historic centre, restricting them to the industrial port in response to a request from UN cultural body UNESCO, due to cruise pollution damaging historic buildings. Amsterdam and Barcelona have done likewise, not only in a bid to curb pollution but also to reduce over-tourism.

The cruise industry, while currently a significant contributor to carbon emissions, shows potential for substantial improvement. The industry argues that the adoption of LNG, exploration of electric technologies, and enhanced energy efficiency practices are steps in the right direction. However, a holistic approach, including better waste management and the use of shore power, is crucial for a truly sustainable transformation.

As technology advances and regulatory pressures increase, the future of cruising could be much greener, offering a more environmentally friendly option for travellers. Meanwhile, tourists conscious of their carbon footprint might consider the type and duration of their cruise, alongside the sustainability practices of the cruise line, when planning their vacations.

Industry, Manufacture and Agriculture

Overall, almost three-quarters of emissions come from energy use; almost one-fifth from agriculture and land *use* [this increases to one-quarter when we include the food system as a whole- including processing, packaging, transport, and retail]; and the remaining 8% from industry and waste.

Energy use in industry: 24.2%

Iron and Steel (7.2%): energy-related emissions from manufacturing iron and steel.

Chemical & petrochemical (3.6%): energy-related emissions from the manufacturing of fertilizers, pharmaceuticals, refrigerants, oil and gas extraction, etc.

Food and tobacco (1%): energy-related emissions from the manufacturing of tobacco products and food processing (the conversion of raw agricultural products into their final products, such as the conversion of wheat into bread).

Non-ferrous metals: 0.7%: non-ferrous metals contain very little iron. They include aluminum, copper, lead, nickel, tin, titanium, zinc, and alloys such as brass. Manufacturing these metals requires energy, which results in emissions.

Paper & pulp (0.6%): energy-related emissions from converting wood into paper and pulp.

Machinery (0.5%): energy-related emissions from the production of machinery.

Other industry (10.6%): energy-related emissions from manufacturing in other industries, including mining and quarrying, construction, textiles, wood products, and transport equipment (such as car manufacturing).

Energy use in buildings: 17.5%

Residential buildings (10.9%): energy-related emissions from electricity generation for lighting, appliances, cooking, etc., and heating at home.

Commercial buildings (6.6%): energy-related emissions from generating electricity for lighting, appliances, etc., and heating in commercial buildings such as offices, restaurants, and shops.

Agriculture and Forestry (18.4%)

Agriculture, Forestry, and Land Use directly account for 18.4% of greenhouse gas emissions. The food system as a whole—including refrigeration, food processing, packaging, and transport—accounts for around one-quarter of greenhouse gas emissions.

Food Emission

The global food system, which encompasses production, and post-farm process such as processing, and distribution is also a key contributor to emissions. It is a problem for which viable technological solutions are not evident although small scale piecemeal improvements, such as methane emissions from cattle may be introduced.

Livestock & fisheries account for 31% of food emissions.

Livestock – animals raised for meat, dairy, eggs and seafood production – contribute to emissions in several ways. Ruminant livestock – mainly cattle – for example, produce methane through their digestive processes (in a process known as 'enteric fermentation'). Manure management, pasture management, and fuel consumption from fishing vessels also fall into this category. This 31% of emissions relates to on-farm 'production' emissions only: it does not include land use change or supply chain emissions from the production of crops for animal feed: these figures are included separately in the other categories.

Crop production accounts for 27% of food emissions.

21% of food's emissions comes from crop production for direct human consumption, and 6% comes from the production of animal feed. They are the direct emissions which result from agricultural production – this includes elements such as the release of nitrous oxide from the application of fertilizers and manure; methane emissions from rice production; and carbon dioxide from agricultural machinery.

Land use accounts for 24% of food emissions.

Twice as many emissions result from land use for livestock (16%) as for crops for human consumption (8%). Agricultural expansion results in the conversion of forests, grasslands and other carbon 'sinks' into cropland or pasture resulting in carbon dioxide emissions. 'Land use' here is the sum of land use change, savannah burning and organic soil cultivation (ploughing and overturning of soils).

Supply chains account for 18% of food emissions.

Food processing (converting produce from the farm into final products), transport, packaging and retail all require energy and resource inputs. Many assume that eating local is key to a low-carbon diet, however, transport emissions are often a very small percentage of food's total emissions – only 6% globally. Whilst supply chain emissions may seem high, at 18%, it's essential for *reducing* emissions by preventing food waste. Food waste emissions are large: one-quarter of emissions (3.3 billion tonnes of CO_2eq) from food production ends up as wastage either from supply chain losses or consumers. Durable packaging, refrigeration and food processing can all help to prevent food waste. For example, wastage of processed fruit and vegetables is 14% lower than fresh, and 8% lower for seafood.[4]

Reducing emissions from food production will be one of the greatest challenges in the coming decades. Unlike many aspects of energy production where viable opportunities for upscaling low-carbon energy are available, the ways in which we can decarbonize agriculture are less clear. We need inputs such as fertilizers to meet growing food demands, and we can't stop cattle from producing methane. We will need a menu of solutions: changes to diets; food waste reduction; improvements in agricultural efficiency; and technologies that make low-carbon food alternatives scalable and affordable.

Monitoring performance is critical and use of the CCPI may prove a useful tool to that end. The Climate Change Performance Index (CCPI) is an annual publication that evaluates and compares the climate protection performance of 60 countries and the European Union, which collectively are responsible for over 90% of global greenhouse gas (GHG) emissions.

Conclusion

This short discussion of Carbon emissions and climate change attempts to identify major issues of concern and the encouragement of remedial measures to reduce the emissions to tolerable levels by 2050- at international and national and local levels, a target recently postponed from 2030 by the UK government.

Over the period 1990 to 2023, carbon dioxide emissions from fossil fuels decreased by 49.5%. Over the same period, primary consumption of fossil fuels dropped by 31.7%. This relatively large decrease in emissions can be attributed to a large decrease in the use of coal accompanied by an increase in the use of gas. Territorial carbon dioxide emissions from gas increased from 26.1% of all carbon dioxide emissions from fossil fuels in the UK in 1990 to 51.2% in 2023, whilst emissions from coal decreased from 38.7% of all fossil fuel carbon dioxide emissions to 2.3% over the same period. Oil was responsible for 35.1% of carbon dioxide emissions from fossil fuels in 1990 and this has increased to 46.4% in 2023. (DESNZ, 2024)

This demonstrates that the UN and many concerned organisations have gone a long way to developing structures and approaches to enable coordinated and progressive responses to achieve the target of zero emissions by the target date. Clearly many countries have delayed, postponed and tinkered with targets and this has been rightly criticised by bodies such as Green Peace and others. There is a need for greater commitment, planning and resource allocation and we all should press upon our MPs and SMPs the need for urgency. Seeking a report on the local situation is appropriate. The Humanist will recognise that in addition to contributing to structural change, the individual also has an important role to play. It is immoral to argue that others are responsible or that science will, unassisted, solve the problems we now face, Examples abound but an obvious structural change is to promote integrated electric public transport and to inhibit unnecessary use of private individual use of cars, in particular. At a personal level, we should try to limit our use of cruise ships, air travel and short car journeys and commit to walking, cycling and public transport where possible. Because domestic energy consumption is such a large element of total energy use, we must also consider practical way of reduction. At a structural level district heating systems should be more efficient than individual consumption. New home must be built to more exacting standards regarding solar installation and insulation. We must secure appropriate insulation measures for our existing homes through cavity wall insulation, double or triple glazing and draft proofing; existing measures while substantial and welcome are too restrictive in respect of government grants and even advice. Use of solar heating and air and ground heat pumps have to be encouraged and adopted where viable. Common Weal provide a valuable analysis of requirement and approaches; something we would all be well to follow (Common Weal, 2024)

Both governments and individuals owe it to the subsequent generations to be bold and committed in supporting, implementing and monitoring the objectives in the Paris Agreement of 2015 and the 17 targets set in the 2030 Sustainable Development Goals.

References

BBC, Earth, Many cruise companies are touting their green credentials. But can cruise ships ever be sustainable?, Isabelle Gerretsen, 28 June 2024

Greenmatch, Can the Large Cruise Ships Drive Systemic Change in Maritime Sustainability?, Inemesit Ukpanah, April, 2024.

Sector by sector: where do global greenhouse gas emissions come from?

UK White Paper, 'The Ten Point Plan for a Green Industrial Revolution', November 2020.

World Health Organisation, 'Climate Change Publications', 2024

Stockholm Environmental Institute, 'Connections between the Paris Agreement and the 2030 Agenda', Working Paper 2023).

Globally, we emit around 50 billion tonnes of greenhouse gases yearly. Where do these emissions come from? We take a look, sector-by-sector, Hannah Ritchie, September 18, 20204.

IPCC (2014): Climate Change 2014: Synthesis Report. Contribution of Working Groups I, II and III to the Fifth Assessment Report of the Intergovernmental Panel on Climate Change [Core Writing Team, R.K. Pachauri and L.A. Meyer (eds.)]. IPCC, Geneva, Switzerland, 151 pp.

Department of Energy Security and Net Zero, '2023 UK greenhouse gas emissions, provisional figures 28 March 2024 Accredited Official Statistics I' 2024.

Hannah Ritchie (2019) - "Food production is responsible for one-quarter of the world's greenhouse gas emissions" Published online at OurWorldInData. org. Retrieved from: 'https://ourworldindata.org/food-ghg-emissions' [Online Resource].

Green News, 'Climate Change in 2024: Where Do We Stand? Global Warming By Stephanie Safdie updated 14 Aug 2024, US Copywriter at Greenly

Wikipedia, Climate change and Global Warming entries, 2024.

International Atomic Energy Agency (IAEA) 'What are SMRs?', November 2021.

Common Weal, 'Green New Deal', -the Common Home Plan, 2024

Stoicism

Introduction

There are many aspects of Stoicism which are reflected in contemporary Humanism. Accordingly, it is instructive to look at some of the tenets underlying the philosophy of the Stoics as a contribution to our understanding. Clearly the influence of the outstanding Greek philosophers namely, Socrates, Plato and Aristotle, are of immense importance in their impact on the development of Christian and Islamic philosophy in particular, as well as present day approaches. Thus Aristotle identified four primary concerns in our approach to living a fulfilling and balanced life, firstly exercise and maintaining health; secondly, emotional equilibrium, thirdly, social integration, humans are social animals and we need to intermingle; and fourthly, we must follow our instincts; we must identify and pursue our interests in learning, creating and expressing ourselves. Such ideas were reflected in Stoic philosophy whose influence was, it can be suggested, equally important in the development of humanist thought.

To explore such, this short chapter now addresses three concerns, firstly the history of Stoicism, secondly what it constitutes and thirdly its current application.

Historical Origins and Development

Stoicism may be classified as having four phases, the Graeco-Roman or early phase, the Christian influence, the Neo-Stoic and the modern phase.

The Graeco-Roman phase comprised three elements. The first comprised three Greek philosophers involved in the founding of Stoicism, namely

Zeno of Citium, born in Cyprus, [334-262 BC]. Zeno founded the sect and was first a pupil of Crates the Cynic.

Cleanthes of Assos [331-232 BC], was the second head of the school and responsible for the concept of the ideal life as one lived in   accordance   with nature, and Chrysippus of Soli [280-207 BC], third leader and possibly most productive of all three having produced 704 books, none of which survive; he had a reputation of a logician and held a cognitive theory of emotions which involved judgement on the value of things; also noted for Chrysippus's dog demonstrating animal intelligence, as explored in the chapter on animal welfare regarding sentience.

The term Stoic was named after the Stoa or Colonnade in Athens; unlike the Academy of Plato or the Lyceum of Aristotle, the Stoics preferred to teach in the open next to the Stoa.

The early phase dominated Greek philosophy after Socrates and Plato and alongside the Cynics and the Epicureans. The cynics were essentially anti-authoritarian and believed in little other than flouting authority, with Diogenes of Synope being a leader of barrel or tub fame. They were largely sceptical of the theoretical approach to philosophy exemplified by Socrates, Plato and Aristotle; perhaps they were the first existentialists. The Epicureans shared a desire to live and promote a 'better life' with the Stoics but were less inclusive- and pantheistic- living in enclaves, apart from the rest of society.

The second period of early Stoicism was dominated by Panaetus [185-110 BC] and Posidonius [135-51BC]. The former developed an eclectic interpretation in his text 'On duties' replicated by in writings by Cicero.

While the third period, and perhaps the most productive, had the significant adherents of Epictetus [c50- c130], a freed slave, Lucius Annaeus Seneca the Younger [4 – 65 AD], the adviser to Emperor Nero, Emperor Marcus Aurelius [121-180 AD] and by Gaius Muconius Rufus [20/30-101 AD], taught by Epictetus.

Epictetus wrote 'Encheiridion', Aurelius wrote 'Meditations', and Seneca various 'Letters' including the 'Shortness of Life'. Rufus wrote various 'Discourses' including reference to regulation of diet, body-care, clothing and even furniture; because none of the original Greek texts survive, these Latin texts, often incorporating excerpts from the founders, are of critical historical importance.

The second phase, the Christian influence, was dominated by St Augustine [354-430 AD] who was eclectic in his references to Stoic texts, as was Thomas Aquinas [1225-1274] in incorporating much of the Stoic approach to reflective self-awareness into his own writings. In truth much of the Christian approach to morality and ethics lent heavily on the Stoic tradition. The third phase, Neo-Stoicism, was initiated largely by the Flemish humanist, Justus Lipsius [1547-1606]. His writings recognised the four Stoic passions to be resisted- greed, joy, fear and sorrow. But God was the master rather than the Stoic belief in pantheism or agnosticism. This influenced Montesquieu, Bacon and Rubens, Rousseau and Hume amongst others.

The fourth contemporary phase of 'Modern Stoicism' is recent and continuing.

It has largely reflected the interest of psychologists and sociologists, perhaps more so than philosophers. In particular Dr. Albert Ellis who developed Rational Emotive Behaviour and Aaron T Beck who was one of the founding fathers of Cognitive Behavioural Therapy.

Stoicism. What is it?

'Physics' was one of the three aspects of the philosophy with logic and ethics being the other two. The Stoics believed in the pervasive power of nature. The world went through cyclical change ending in fire which was also seen as a spiritual element in which we would be consumed before a rebirth of the world in a changing cosmos. If 'God' existed, this was seen as a holistic entity comprising the cosmos; pantheism was a linked belief.

The world, it was said, is a benign entity governed for the best. Any consideration of imperfection arises from seeing ourselves in relative isolation rather than being part of the whole- as a foot being part of the body. The changes experienced in the cosmos are pre-ordained, but this does not relieve us from responsibility for our actions.

The cosmos and the world were seen as being guided by rational and benign change and it was imperative to enjoy the moment not only of pleasant times but also of the more seemingly hurtful aspects of experience. The objective was to control the 'emotions' to achieve a tranquil state of equilibrium with 'nature'. Marcus Aurelius 'constantly regard the universe as one living being. Reason is the foundation of humanity and the universe. The goal of life is to live according to reason and in accordance with nature.'

Eudaimonia, or the Greek concept of happiness or flourishing, is found in accepting the moment as it presents itself. Happiness is seen as achieved through a fulfilling and fruitful life rather than a narrow sense of personal enjoyment. Accordingly, the social aspect of mutual support, artistic endeavour and physical activity are part of the Stoic package.

While being 'Stoical' included a kind of dogged endurance of difficulties, there was no expectation of self-denial in the sense that achieving wealth was not unvirtuous, provided this was done with honesty and rational insight. Zeno himself was a successful merchant, Seneca well off and Marcus Aurelius enjoyed the benefits of being Emperor.

The need for reflection recognised meditation as of benefit and this aspect of philosophical belief was shared with Buddhism. There was no belief in reincarnation.

There was a general belief in the equality of the sexes- as illustrated by Rufus's lectures on the subject. Seneca observed 'he whom you call a slave sprang from the same stock, is smiled upon by the same skies, and, on equal terms as yourself, breathes, lives and dies.' While the Christian church generally thought of the Stoics as pagans, it adopted many of its concepts in its doctrines such as logos or logic and virtue in the absence of passion. Similarly, the Eastern and Orthodox churches accepted the Stoic ideal of 'dispassion'. The Stoic should be indifferent to the vicissitudes of life in the sense of being unconcerned with those aspects of living over which we have no control or influence but should focus on those which he or she may affect.

As Epictetus questioned, 'Show me who is sick and yet happy, in peril and yet happy, dying and yet happy. In exile and happy. Show me him. By the Gods, I would fain see a Stoic'.

What was under control, however, would include one's fears and appetites and desires and hopes. This Stoic outlook remained central to Western culture as the basis of educated sentiment. However, Adam Smith in his 'Moral Sentiments' observed the pursuit of Stoic Indifference may become a celebration of apathy. That view is questioned by modern adherents.

Stoicism Today

Because of its emphasis on logic, rational thought and the encouragement of reflective contemplation, there appears to be a timelessness about Stoic philosophy. One could argue that such a view contrasts with the irrational and emotive outbursts of leading politicians such as Viktor Orban, Vlademir Putin and Donald Trump today but chimes with contemporary interests in mindfulness, social tolerance of difference and the benefits of periods of retreat. Moreover, the very troubling developments of the wars in the Ukraine, in Gaza, in the Sudan and in the Yemen and also climate change would suggest that a Stoic approach might reap some benefits. Firstly, there is the acceptance of the appropriateness of human intervention to save life and secure equitable governance and secondly the need to accept change when inevitable and then make the most of the resultant conditions.

There may also be particular benefits perceived for those of differing circumstances and abilities and for the aged and infirm given the emphasis on positive thinking about making the most of challenging situations.

References

Wikipedia; Entries on Stoicism

Routledge Shorter Encyclopedia of Philosophy, Routledge; Entry on Stoicism

Bertrand Russell, The History of Western Philosophy, 260-276, Allen and Unwin, 1961

A C Grayling, Ideas that Matter,181-2 Phoenix, 2009

Steven M, Cahn, Classics of Western Philosophy, 3rd Edition, 1990

Entries on Plato, from 1-112, Aristotle, 193-216, Epictetus, 323- 342, Augustine, 342-362, Aquinas, 383-402.

Simon Blackburn, Oxford Dictionary of Philosophy, Entry on Stoicism 383-4, Oxford University Press, 1994

Mind and Body; Determinism and Free Will

There is a long history of discussion concerning the relationship between the human mind and body.

Renee Descartes (1596-1650) in advocating that the body was separate from the conscious mind promoted the concept of dualism which, in turn, underpinned the belief that spirituality and the belief in god created consciousness as a separate entity from the body itself. Such dualism was challenged by a growth in scientific knowledge about the body and its workings. Thus monism, a belief that the mind and body were a single entity, was manifest in materialist notions which also became known as physicalist.

In general, the *existence* of these mind–body connections seem unproblematic. Issues arise, however, once one considers what exactly we should make of these relations from a scientific perspective. Such reflections raise a number of questions like:

- Are the mind and body two distinct entities, or a single entity?
- Are the mind and brain the same>
- If the mind and body are two distinct entities, is it possible for the two of them causally to interact?
- If so, what is the nature of this interaction and is it a subject for empirical study?
- If the mind and body are a single entity, then are mental events explicable in terms of physical events, or vice versa?

These and other questions that discuss the relation between mind and body are questions that all fall under the banner of the 'mind–body problem'. In examining such issues, it may be instructive to describe in brief ideas of some of the major contributors to this debate, namely, Rene Descartes, David Hume, Immanuel Kant, Thomas Huxley, AN Whitehead, Karl Popper, and Gilbert Ryle and John Searle. Wikipedia provides helpful articles on each of these. The following attempts to summarise the main points.

Rene Descartes

Descartes (1596–1650) believed that the mind exerted control over the brain *via* the pineal gland.

'My view is that this gland is the principal seat of the soul, and the place in which all our thoughts are formed'. René Descartes, Treatise of Man

'[The] mechanism of our body is so constructed that simply by this gland's being moved in any way by the soul or by any other cause, it drives the surrounding spirits towards the pores of the brain, which direct them through the nerves to the muscles; and in this way the gland makes the spirits move the limbs'. René Descartes' Passions of the Soul.

His concept of relation between mind and body is called Cartesian dualism. He held that *mind* was distinct from *matter* but could influence matter. How such an interaction could be exerted remains a contentious issue.

David Hume

For Hume (1711-1776) the self is not an entity because there was no specific impression corresponding to 'I', that the status of self was no more than a bundle of sensations. Accordingly, he would be classified as a compatibilist, in the sense that while the mind was a physical entity as part of the body and subject to the laws of causation, this did not void the idea of free will.

It was Hume's 'Enquiry Concerning Human Understanding' [1748] which awakened Kant, he admitted, from his dogmatic slumbers.

Immanuel Kant

For Kant (1724-1804) beyond mind and matter exists a world of a priori forms which are seen as necessary preconditions for understanding. Some of these forms, space and time being examples, today seem to be preprogrammed into the brain akin to intuition.

'…whatever it is that impinges on us from the mind-independent world does not come in a spatial or a temporal matrix… The mind has two pure forms of intuition built into it to allow it to… organise this manifold of raw intuition.'

Kant views the mind and body interaction as taking place through forces that may be of different kinds for mind and body.

Thomas Huxley

For Thomas Huxley (1825–1895) the conscious mind was a by-product of the brain that has no influence upon the brain, a so-called epiphenomenon

On the epiphenomenalist view, mental events play no causal role. Huxley compared mental events to a steam whistle that contributes nothing to the work of a locomotive.

A.N. Whitehead

Whitehead (1861-1947) advocated a sophisticated form of panpsychism. This is a form of animism deriving from a belief that all things, whether living or inanimate, are imbued with some kind of spiritual or psychological presence. Perhaps this may be akin to the understanding that some animals, the octopus being a prime example, have sensory perceptions in their tentacles that can act independently of the central nervous system.

Karl Popper

For Popper (1902–1994) there are three aspects of the mind–body problem: the worlds of 1. matter, 2. mind, and 3. the creations of the mind, such as physics or mathematics. In his view, the third-world creations of the mind could be interpreted by the second-world mind and used to affect the first world of matter.

The body–mind problem is the question of whether and how our thought processes in World 2 are bound up with brain events in World 1. ...I would argue that the first and oldest of these attempted solutions is the only one that deserves to be taken seriously [namely]: World 2 and World 1 interact, so that when someone reads a book or listens to a lecture, brain events occur that *act* upon the World 2 of the reader's or listener's thoughts; and conversely, when a mathematician follows a proof, his World 2 *acts* upon his brain and thus upon World 1. This, then, is the thesis of body–mind interaction.

—◻Karl Popper, Notes of a realist on the body–mind problem

Gilbert Ryle

With his 1949 book, The Concept of Mind, Ryle (1900-1976) "was seen to have put the final nail in the coffin of Cartesian dualism".

In the chapter "Descartes' Myth," Ryle introduces "the dogma of the Ghost in the machine" to describe the philosophical concept of the mind as an entity separate from the body:

I hope to prove that it is entirely false, and false not in detail but in principle. It is not merely an assemblage of particular mistakes. It is one big mistake and a mistake of a special kind. It is, namely, a category mistake.

John Searle

According to John Searle (1932-) there is no more a mind–body problem than there is a macro–micro economics problem. They are different levels of description of the same set of phenomena. But Searle maintains that the mental – the domain of qualitative experience and understanding – is autonomous and has no counterpart on the micro-level; Joshua Rust, John Searl (2009)

A number of problems arise from these explanations, which is for the most part Cartesian dualism and materialism or physicalism. With reference to the former, the absent of evidence relating to a belief in God or spiritualism as a separate entity undermined the early explanation of dualism.

However, it is not easy to see how the concepts of mind and body relate. To a large extent a belief in materialism was consistent with Newtonian ideas about the physical world, in the sense that all actions were dependent on a cause or causes. Consequently, human action would be dependent on identifiable input whether through genetic, social, behavioural or physical in nature. This conclusion appeared to challenge the idea that humans exercise independent agency in determining their actions or even their thoughts. For the materialist, everything including the brain is constructed from physical matter, even to the extent of atoms colliding with each other, and consciousness is a mere inactive by-product of these neural processes or epiphenomena. Such processes are the essential drivers of thoughts and decisions leading to actions. Accordingly conscious and independent agency plays little if any part in this process.

This belief in causality is underpinned by an exclusion of any action being initiated independently. The brain is merely a complicated biological machine which requires nothing beyond the external stimulus described in making decisions. Accordingly, the brain machine makes human choices and actions inevitable and consequently predictable.

Free Will

If this materialist view is credible then the question arises to what room it leaves for individual agency in decision making and action. This has immense implications. If our decisions and actions are predetermined and originate from causes over which we have little if any control, such a conclusion negates any sense of responsibility for our actions, and our ability to make informed choices and judgments.

However, we have an embedded sense of awareness concerning freedom of action. In a physical sense, we have freedom to walk, to run, to talk, to sit down, to participate in activities and to refrain from doing so according to our desires and beliefs. We believe that there is a genuine choice in taking one option rather than another and we also feel that we are consciously making such decisions rather than being driven to them.

Our belief in freedom of action is of fundamental importance. We believe that as intelligent animals we are not controlled entirely by instinct, but we retain a conscious free agency as part of our ability to survive that may well be part of a Darwinian process of evolution. Moreover, free will is a prerequisite for moral responsibility and the development of interpersonal responsiveness in a civilized society. Thus, our system of law and order in both criminal and civil matters is dependent on free will. The criminal law and prison regimes, the concept of democratic politics and the law of contract are examples of our dependence on free agency.

Some have argued that in order to make sense of free will we have to abandon talk of choices being made by our brains or our minds or our rational or conscious selves. The agents of choice, it is argued, comprise a holistic idea of 'us'. Decisions are made consciously on occasion and sometimes unconsciously; sometimes automatically and sometimes on the basis of thought after considering rational options and sometimes on the basis of emotion or instinct.

Another possible paradigm was being promoted by the compatibilist philosopher Simon Blackburn (2008) who expressed the idea of a flexible agency which avoided the extremes of hard determinism [the absence of real choice] and supernatural interventionism. The brain he argues has various modules for information processing comparable to a computer software process where choices are enabled. Thus, we may consider possibilities of action informed by our knowledge, understanding and our deliberation. And we may be seen as part and parcel of the causal order of events and thus enabled to make a genuine choice in decision making. In such an analysis, we remain responsible for our actions, good or bad.

The above information producer theory may not be too far from the complexity theory. This theory argues that a complex system is composed of many different systems that interact and produce emergent properties. Mind and consciousness are emergent properties arising from the processes of the brain. These properties are not found at the fundamental physical level. This explains how it can be that beliefs, desires and intentions can actually change things without us having to postulate any supernatural or non-physical will or soul. As Gazzinger (2012) suggests, mental states such as beliefs thoughts and desires all arise from brain activity and these in turn can influence our decisions to act in one way for another.

Both complexity theory and the theory of emergent consciousness conclude that free will is not an illusion. Our thoughts really do change what we do. Again, both these theories appear compatibilist with interactionist theories which contend that just as our physical state may influence our thinking and the activity of the mind so our thinking and mind activity may determine our physical response.

Another compatibilist theory allowing for the exercise of free will, is the uncertainty principle or chaos theory. The chaos theory, or the butterfly effect, argues that very minor changes can lead to very large and different final outcomes. There is some doubt however whether this inevitably challenges the determinist theory of cause and effect.

However, the uncertainty principle asserts that there is a fundamental indeterminacy in our knowledge about physical particles. It is true however that both choice uncertainty and indeterminacy do not directly address or solve the problem of free will.

Unless we wish to describe ourselves as victims of the doctrine of cause and effect in which we have no agency to guide, control or otherwise to affect our thoughts and actions, then we are likely to conclude that the concept of free will permits us to follow our beliefs and to exercise judgment and discretion in determining our thoughts and actions.

Consequently, we have a responsibility to ourselves and our fellow citizens to act rationally and to act with consideration to others. The Humanist code, as a result, remains alive and ticking, if not positively kicking.

References

Unpublished Paper 'The Problem of Free Will', 2022
Julian Baggini, 'Freedom Regained', Granta Books, 2015
Julian Baggini, 'The Ego Trick,' Granta, 2011
Gazzaniga, 'Who's in Charge', Robinson, 2012
Gregory Richard (ed.), 'The Oxford Companion to the Mind', Oxford University Press, 1987
Joshua Rust, John Seale, Bloomsbury, 2009
Davis Chalmers, 'The Conscious Mind', Oxford University Press, 1996

Simon Blackburn, 'The Oxford Dictionary of Philosophy. Oxford University Press, 2008

Sam Harris, Free Will, Deckle Edge, 2012.

Wikipedia [articles as underlined above] and Epiphenomenalism.

Pinker, Steven, Enlightenment Now, Penguin Books, 2019

Tullis, Raymond, Does the Cosmos Have a Purpose? Philosophy Now, Issue 162, June/July, 2024.

Just War, or just war?

Introduction

With the invasion of the Ukraine by Russia and the taking of Israeli hostages by Hamas followed by over 35,000 civilian deaths in Gaza, we are reminded of the fragility of peace and the dangers of war. Such is exacerbated by the threat of regional expansion and indeed of nuclear war, leading to worldwide destruction. With such threats we are rightly reminded of the need to examine whether or not we are, or should be, guided by the morality and ethics relating to warfare.

The idea behind this exploratory excursion is to identify what the ethics may be behind 'legitimate war', its origin, conduct and aftermath, and how we might interpose our own notions of justice and fairness in these and like tragic developments.

Historical Development

In China in the pre-Christian era, warring factions between the 10 or more 'states' led to the deployment of sophisticated strategies as exemplified by Sun Tzi in his treatise' On War' (472 BC). This work was later referred to by Mao Zedong in his strategies against the Nationalists and these strategies extended their influence to politics and finance. Sun Tzi emphasised the need to understand the enemy and even allowed for temporary 'defeat' to avoid loss of life.

In his De re Publica and de Officiis, Cicero, acknowledging the Stoic influence, discusses the conditions that must exist before a war is justly commenced and waged. He laid the groundwork for many of the principles of the later just war tradition. However, his justification of war for the sake of glory conflicts with the Stoic view found in Panaetius (185-110) in relation to the legal and religious principles.

St. Augustine (354-430) addressed the theory of 'the just war' laying the foundations for Thomas Aquinus (1224-1274) who, in his Summa Theologicae, held that war must be declared and conducted by a competent authority, i.e. the ruler or sovereign of the state concerned. It must be fought to promote good and avoid evil with a view to restoring peace and justice when over. War against a tyrannical regime is potentially just, but the stability of the state is emphasised.

Carl Von Clausewitz, a Prussian General, (1780-1831) was considered one of the most influential war strategists and tacticians. In his classic strategic treatise 'On War' (1832, the revised edition published posthumously), Clausewitz emphasizes the uncertainty under which all generals and statesmen labour (known as the "fog of war") and the tendency for any plan, no matter how simple, to go awry. Periodically, it could be argued, there have been geniuses who could steer a war from beginning to end, but in most cases, wars have been shaped by a group of Generals and or Committees. And, as Clausewitz says in an introductory note to 'On War', "When it is not a question of acting oneself but of persuading others in discussion, the need is for clear ideas and the ability to show their connection with each other". The concept of total war resulting in devastating loss to achieve quick gains and perhaps lessening the length of war have been attributed to him.

Historically the reasons for conflict are multifarious. Christian Religious rivalry between Sunnis and Shiites, between Catholics and Protestants between Muslims and Christians, between Hindus and Christians or Muslims. Disputed boundaries, as in Kashmir, Empire building, as with Napoleon, ethnic conflict. as in the Biafran war, annexation of territory as a defensive or pre-emptive move, as with Crimea, breach of treaties, as in World War1. Monetary/material gain, protection of minorities against human rights violations and prevention of genocide are further examples.

It could we argued that very few of the historical wars were justified in terms of just war theory although WW2 waged between an exploitative, racist, tyrannical, genocidal and expansionist regime may be an exception.

The Concept of Just War

The idea of just war, or bellum iustum, comprises three components; firstly, that relating to the initiation of war, the right to go to war or, ius ad bellum, secondly the rights or obligations relating to the conduct of war itself, ius in bello, and thirdly, a later edition, ius post bellum.

The just war tradition -a set of mutually agreed rules of combat- may be said to commonly evolve between two culturally similar enemies. That is, when an array of values is shared between two warring peoples, we often find that they implicitly or explicitly agree upon limits to their warfare. But when enemies differ greatly because of different religious beliefs, race, or language or even geography and as such they see each other as "less than human", war conventions are rarely applied. It is only when the enemy is seen to be a people sharing a moral identity with whom one will do business in the following peace, that tacit or explicit rules are formed for how wars should be fought and who they should involve and what kind of relations should apply in the aftermath of war. In part, the motivation for forming or agreeing to certain conventions, can be seen as mutually benefiting-preferable, for instance, to the deployment of any underhand tactics or weapons that may provoke an indefinite series of vengeance acts, or the kinds of action that have proved to be detrimental to the political or moral interests to both sides in the past.

Ziyad Hayatli (2018) has identified key elements in the philosophy of war, as noted below. Firstly, a term such as 'the laws of war' seems oxymoronic [or even moronic] in nature: a contradiction in terms. On the one hand, law is a rigid structure of rules that is associated with order; on the other hand, war is an activity characterised by chaos and destruction. Yet there is now an understanding that when one goes to war, certain behaviours are expected, and when these standards are violated, demands for international justice are broadcast on the air, written in the papers, and shouted through the megaphones [perhaps, mobilised through the mobiles may be more apposite]. Institutions such as the United Nations are chided as toothless and useless due to their limitations. The International Criminal Court is caught up in the debates about the laws and lawfulness of war, and they are numerous, concerning drone warfare, artificial intelligence, collateral damage, winning hearts and minds, chemical and biological weapons, the need for nuclear deterrence, and the very idea of humanitarian military intervention.

Over the centuries attitudes relating to the justification of war and it's conduct extend to the natural law theories of the Middle Ages, which described a substantial just war doctrine, and then, in the period of the 18th century Enlightenment, new conceptions of state and sovereignty would change the idea of war. It emphasised that ideas about the nature of war are closely tied to conceptions of what a state is, and how states relate to one another. Western philosophy generally assumed that morality was an inherent characteristic of mankind as a gift from God, known as Natural Laws. With regard to the laws of war, scholastics and theologians from Thomas Aquinas (1225-1274) to Hugo Grotius (1583-1645) developed a substantial doctrine of 'Just War Theory' – a theory of when waging war was just, and when it was unjust (ius ad bellum'), as well as what sort of behaviour was just within war ('ius in bello').

Hugo Grotius published his seminal work De iure Belli ac Pacis (The Law of War and Peace) in 1629. Europe, was embattled at this time in the Thirty Years' War, in which Catholic and Protestant states were warring against one another. In this work Grotius described the political order as a loose international society. He also explored the basic idea of self-defence as a lawful use of force, on both the private and the state level. His insights earned him the title 'the father of international law'. Most importantly, Grotius made recommendations which showed a remarkable amount of tolerance, given the then political climate. One was that war waged against others merely because of their different interpretation of Christianity is unjust. The end of the Thirty Years' War in 1648 saw the adoption of this and other recommendations in what became known as the Peace of Westphalia, by which much of Europe was transformed from a group of hierarchical states. Questions arose how a state could be so negligent towards its own soldiers once they are of 'no use' and argued for the importance of principles when fighting wars. It also emphasised the idea of preventing needless suffering. To Henry Dunant, a combatant was an agent of the state, fulfilling a duty delegated by that state, and when that combatant is wounded to the point that they're no longer able to fulfil that duty, they cease to become such agents. There is no further point in killing, maiming, or torturing them. While war may be unpreventable, the suffering therein can and should be constrained.

Military targets, it was argued, must be distinguished from non-targets. This rule was already present in Christian and Islamic traditions but the ICRC [International Committee of the Red Cross] reinvigorated and promulgated the distinction between military and non-military in a more modern and global context. Now, the ICRC considers it as a core principle.

This philosophy of war views the state as an intangible entity composed of agents who fulfil its interests at every level, from soldiers to civil servants and law-makers. Given that the concept of the state has been closely linked with philosophies of war (both *ad bellum* and *in bello*), the second half of the Twentieth Century would bring about fresh challenges.

The Twentieth Century and the Future

Second World War changed the world order in that Grotius's idea of a loose international society really came to fruition with the subsequent creation of the United Nations in 1945. The new global community of states sought to make certain behaviours unlawful. Wars required a legitimate purpose and Wars of aggression and expansionism, therefore, became unacceptable. Officially, war became permissible in only two circumstances: self-defence, or by a binding resolution from the Security Council. Chapter VII of *The United Nations Charter* in its entirety, and particularly Article 51, makes this point very clearly. But the so-called 'global society of states' has found loopholes. And the new world of decolonisation, national liberation, human rights treaties, and sovereign state self-determination introduced a new kind of entity onto the international field – 'territorial non-state actors'. These were organisations that closely resembled states, but were not quite states. They're perfect vessels for states to engage in proxy warfare, where neither side directly engages the other. Now arguing for humanitarian intervention became the new tactic.

As we have observed for a long time the concept of warfare had been wedded to the concept of the state, but as territorial non-state actors became a significant part of the world of war, this no longer holds true. Terms such as 'terrorism' and 'freedom fighter' entered everyone's lexicon. And no discussion of war is complete without mentioning the 'War on Terror'. The challenge of developing a new philosophy where combatants include not only the functionary of states but also terrorists or freedom fighters is very real. The late international legal scholar Antonio Cassese (2013) called this the 'Freedom Fighter's Problem'. Are terrorists, or 'combatants of a non-state actor', different to the soldiers of a conventional army? If so, how and why? Do we restrict human rights in the face of such an enemy, for the sake of national security? Or would the reduction of human rights have a worsening effect? These debates are of current significance. Cassese himself explored how the word 'terrorism' is sometimes used in a manipulative way that merely reflects a state's interests. This is not to say that terrorism is not a real threat or a genuine phenomenon.

The conflict in Syria is emblematic of this new world of war. It has truly tested the morality of combatants, observers, and political commentators. Accusations of human rights abuses, child conscription, and war by proxy fly around. On the one hand there is a despotic, merciless tyrant; on the other rebels, some of whom have highly questionable beliefs and patrons. The tyrant stands up to global imperialism and proxy warfare from the 'hypocritical West'; yet the rebels stand up to 'tyranny' and 'despotism'. Clearly Hamas, without the child conscription accusation, may similarly test our moral concerns. Moreover, the issues of statehood regarding Palestine raise further issues relating to identity and accountability. Israel may not meet the description of a despotic tyrant, given its democratic status, but unrelenting, merciless, ruthless and indifferent to the deaths of non-combatants are accusations based on the reality of the conflict. Moreover, its separate development in expanded settlements in Palestinian as well as denial of equal status to Palestinian denizens, appropriation of land and denial of Arab land rights are clear evidence of unjust treatment based on ethnicity.

The Jus Ad Bellum Convention

These are the rules for when it is just to go to war.
(1) Does the war have Just Authority (*Auctoritas*)?
(2) Does the war have Just Cause (*Causa*)?
(3) Is the war being started with the Right Intentions (*Intentio*)?
(4) Is the proposed military action proportional to the situation?
(5) Is there a good probability of success in achieving the war's aims
(6) Peaceful alternatives must all have been exhausted first.

The principles of the justice of war are commonly held to be: having just cause, being a last resort, being declared by a proper authority, possessing right intention, having a reasonable chance of success, and the end being proportional to the means used. One can immediately detect that the principles are not wholly deontological nor consequentialist—they invoke the concerns of both models. Whilst this provides just war theory with the advantage of flexibility, the lack of a strict ethical framework means that the principles themselves are open to broad interpretations. Examining each in turn draws attention to the relevant problems.

The Principles of Jus In Bello

These are the rules guiding behaviour once a war has started.

The rules of just conduct within war fall under the two broad principles of discrimination and proportionality. The principle of discrimination concerns who are legitimate targets in war, whilst the principle of proportionality concerns how much force is morally appropriate. A third principle can be added to the traditional two, namely the principle of responsibility, which demands an examination of where responsibility lies in war.
(1) Discrimination: no violence towards civilians, or combatants who have surrendered.
(2) Proportionality: harm to lives or property must not be disproportionate to the military advantage expected to be gained.

(3) Responsibility: Every individual, regardless of rank, is personally responsible for any war crime that he might commit. Soldiers must refuse to obey any orders that they know to be immoral.

(4) No use of certain unacceptable weapons and tactics (e.g. rape, or forcing captives to fight their own side, or biological weapons).

Jus Post Bellum

Following the cessation of a war, three possibilities emerge: either the army has been defeated, has been victorious, or it has agreed to a ceasefire. Principles of justice may then be applied to each situation. Orend presents a useful summary of the principles of *jus post bellum* : the principle of discrimination should be employed to avoid imposing punishment on innocents or non-combatants; the rights or traditions of the defeated deserve respect; the claims of victory should be proportional to the war's character; compensatory claims should be tempered by the principles of discrimination and proportionality; and, controversially, the need to rehabilitate or re-educate an aggressor should also be considered.

It has often been remarked that justice, like history, is written by the victors. A defeated army and indeed the civilian body from which the army stems should thus be prepared to subject itself to the imposition of rules and forms of punishments, humiliation, and even retributions that it would not otherwise agree to. The lives, values, and resources that have been fought for must now be handed over to the conquerors.

Brian Orend (2001) presents a useful summary of the principles of jus post bellum : the principle of discrimination should be employed to avoid imposing punishment on innocents or non-combatants; the rights or traditions of the defeated deserve respect; the claims of victory should be proportional to the war's character; compensatory claims should be tempered by the principles of discrimination and proportionality; and, controversially, the need to rehabilitate or re-educate an aggressor should also be considered.

Geneva Conventions and Protocols

While the principles relating to the commencement of war, its conduct and the aftermath may influence the behaviour of combatants, legal conventions impose obligations which may result in criminal penalties and as a result may be seen as more onerous and require more profound scrutiny and observance.

The most important of these are the Geneva Conventions, namely the four conventions of 1949 and the two protocols of 1977.

The development of these provisions stemmed from the work of Henri Dunant, the founder of the Red Cross, who initiated international negotiations leading to the first Convention of 1864 for the amelioration of the war wounded. This provided for

1. The immunity from capture and destruction of all for establishments the treatment of wounded and sicked soldiers and their personnel.
2. The impartial reception and treatment of all combatants.
3. The protection of civilians by providing aid to the wounded.
4. The recognition of the red cross symbol as a means of identifying relevant personnel and equipment.

These provisions were amended and extended in 1906, and 1929 which latter related to humane treatment of prisoners, the furnishing of information and official visits to camps by representatives of neutral states.

Because some of the belligerents in WW2 has abused some of the principles, an International Red Cross conference was held in Stockholm in 1948. This conference developed four conventions approved in Geneva the following year, 1949.

These conventions built on the earlier provisions: -

1. They define the rights of war prisoners, civilians and military personnel around a war zone.
2. they provide protection for the wounded and sick.
3. they define the rights and protections afforded to non-combatants who meet the criteria of protected persons.

While the Geneva Conventions and protocols addressed the treatment of prisoners and those wounded as well as those assigned for their welfare, it is the Hague Conventions which deal with the conduct of warfare itself.

The Hague Conventions

The Hague Conventions of 1899 and 1907 were based on the Lieber Code.

The first Convention comprised three main treaties and three additional declarations,

The latter provides by Article 1 that the contracting parties agree that hostilities between themselves must not commence without previous and explicit warning, in the form of either a Declaration of war, giving reasons, or an ultimatum with conditional declaration,

1.The first related to the pacific settlement of disputes and created the Permanent Court of Arbitration which survives to this day.

2. The second relates to the law and customs of wars on land, incorporates the Geneva Convention of 1864, as outlined above, forbids the use of poisons, looting, the bombardment of undefended towns or settlements, the collective punishment of prisoners and enforced military service of residents in occupied territory.

3.The third convention relates to maritime warfare and incorporates similar provision as above.

The three additional declarations relate to

1. the prohibition of the discharge of projectiles and explosives from balloons
2. the prohibition of the deployment of poisonous gases
3. this bans the use of certain bullets which expand on impact.

The Convention of 1907; this convention consists of some thirteen treaties, eight of which relate to maritime warfare. The remainder cover war declaration and related reparation liability, limitation of hostilities for recovering debt, respecting the law and customs relating to land war and the rights and duties of neutral powers and persons regarding land war.

The Geneva protocol which came into effect in 1928, considered part of the Hague Conventions banned, permanently, the use of chemical and biological warfare.

Enforcement

Many of the above Conventions and Declarations were violated in WW1. The invasion of Luxembourg and Belgium in 1914 was a violation of Convention V of 1907 which prohibits the violation of neutral territory which was done to contain France. Moreover, poison gas was used by the combatants throughout the war, another clear violation of the Conventions.

After WW2, a military Tribunal was convened at Nuremberg for the trial of German war criminals. The judges found that be the time of the WW2 the rules laid down by the conventions relating to the customs of war were recognised by all 'civilised' nations. Consequently, a country need not have signed and ratified the conventions in order to be bound by them. While many of the then current provisions of these treaties have been modified and, or, extended by subsequent provision, that ruling binds all countries and combatants to comply with the accepted customs of war, or to face the courts and their judgments.

From its establishment in 2002, the ICC or International Criminal Court, an intergovernmental court based in the Hague, has been the principal court with jurisdiction over was crimes. It is the first and only international court with jurisdiction to hold individuals accountable. However, a number of major states have not signed up and recognised the Court's jurisdiction; these include China, Russia, India, Israel and the US. However, the ICC's ongoing investigations into alleged war crimes, in the Ukraine, including arrest warrants for Putin and others, and the Israel-Hamas war remain a critical test for the Court's authority. The International Court of Justice is an organ of the UN which hears disputes between states and was founded in 1945, commencing a year later; it is the only UN organ based outside the USA and is based in the Hague. The opportunity for third-party states to seek remedies or sanctions against non-national Human Rights offenders is limited but the US Magnitsky Act of 2012, followed by like legislation in 29 Countries by the end of 2023 has enabled the freezing of monies held by Human Rights violators in addition to banning their entry to the relevant country. Unsurprisingly, Putin expressed his rabid opposition to this.

Russia and Ukraine

Is it possible to justify the invasion, given the above conditions and legal constraints? Vladimir Putin, and his government, authorised the invasion. Is this just authority? Even if the legitimacy of the election of the President and his government is subject to challenge, prima facie, the invasion appears to be authorised from a legitimate authority. However, there was no ultimatum nor stated reason for invasion before it took place.

Does the war have just cause? The Russian Government refer to a number of reasons justifying the invasion but after it took place. There are a number of pro Russian controlled strongholds in Donesk whose allegiance to the Ukraine government was dubious. The Russian Government claimed that the Ukraine Government was led by Nazis. Irrespective of the truth or otherwise of the Russian narrative, in the absence of dispute regarding legitimate borders of Ukraine this argument as well as the alleged threat of Ukraine becoming a member of NATO could not be seen as justifying an invasion, or military operations, as Russian news reporters as well as the population at large were obliged to describe it. Moreover, there was no evidence that this invasion could be seen as a last resort, given the absence of dialogue over identified and verified grievances.

Was the war started with the right intentions? Ambiguous as this condition may be, the evident intention of the war was to annex the Ukraine as part of the Russian State. Putin had made clear that he rued Yeltsin's decision to relinquish authority over the Soviet Union's previous controlled states, and in particular Latvia, Estonia, Lithuania as well as the Ukraine. But such regret does not justify war as just cause nor with justifiable intentions.

The reasonable likelihood of success is more open ended. Given the resources available both in respect of troops and armaments to Russia and, without foreign intervention, the limited resources available to the Ukraine, the prospects of Russian success may have seemed reasonable from the commencement. Given the developments, that optimism may have been misplaced but there is still a prospect of victory through attrition. Such, however, does nothing to justify the invasion.

On the basis of the above, there is no legitimate reason, under the Ius Ad Bellum convention for the Russian invasion.

Has the war been conducted in a just manner?

According to Wikipedia, since the invasion in 2022 the Russian Military and authorities have committed war crimes on a significant scale. These include deliberate attacks on civilian targets, including hospitals and the Nuclear power grid, indiscriminate attacks on densely populated areas, including cluster bombs, torture and murder of civilians, forced deportation, sexual assaults including rape of women and children, destruction of cultural heritage, and the murder, torture and mutilation of prisoners.

As a consequence, the Prosecutor for the International Criminal Court in March 2023 opened a full investigation into past, from 21 November 2013, and present war crimes, crimes against Humanity and Genocide committed in Ukraine. This period would cover the invasion and annexation of Crimea. In addition, two other agencies are now involved in collating information relating to alleged war crimes, namely the Independent International Commission of Inquiry on Ukraine, set up by the UN Human Rights Council, and the UN Human Rights Monitoring Mission, set up by the UN High Commission for Human Rights.

By October 2024, the Prosecutor's office had documented almost 40,000 alleged Russian War crimes, identified 600 suspects and initiated proceedings against 80.

But it is evident that it is most unlikely that Russia or it's war criminals including Putin will be put on trial or otherwise called to account. Clearly the overriding strength in depth of Russia, as well as its geographical extent means that it is likely to withstand military losses, however persistent. As a result, even if Ukraine wins a tactical victory, this will not mean an unsustainable material loss or defeat for the Russian State. This despite the evident loss of life for conscripted inmates, Chechnyan volunteers (12,000, Kadyrov, 2022) as well as Russian Nationals. As of June 2024, 3,642 Russian officers and 3,997 Ukrainian officers had been killed, and the OHCHR verified 29,732 civilian casualties of which a third were dead and the actual numbers likely to be higher. According to the UNHCR 3.7 million people are currently displaced and 5.9 million refugees and asylum seekers spread across the European region, (some 80% being women and children).

Even if the war results in a change of Government- and there are vested interests against such change- this does not entail individual or collective calling to account nor the willingness to accept restitution for the very significant loss in life and structure inflicted on Ukraine. No third power would be likely to intervene and demand otherwise without the threat of further military conflict; this is something neither NATO nor individual powers would sanction. Russia has already survived a significant number of economic sanctions and further sanctions are unlikely to change attitudes or options.

Such a conclusion not only challenges the purpose and effect of treaties and legal agreements relating to warfare, but also has the appearance of acquiescence in unjust peace should that eventuate.

Is this also true of the experience in Israel and Gaza?

The Israel and Gaza/Palestine Conflict

The creation of the State of Israel is not without controversy. While accepting the justifiable grievances of the Palestinian land owners and residents about their subjection to land grab without compensation, arbitration or restitution, our starting point is to assume, on the first hand, the right of Israel to exist and, on the other hand the right, of the Palestine community to have a recognised independent state, to have claims for land recovery and compensation recognised.

But the purpose of the present debate is to focus on the Hamas raid of 7 October 2023 and the aftermath.

The raid by Hamas and several other groups of Palestinians was the first incursion into Israeli land since the 1948 Arab-Israeli war. After a barrage of some 3,000 rockets, Hamas fighters breached the border, attacked military bases and killed civilians in 21 communities. The IDF estimated that about 3,000 militants had invaded with later incursions from civilians. The attackers killed 1,139 people including 695 civilians, 38 being children, 71 foreign nationals and 373 of the security forces. About 250 Israeli soldiers and civilians, including 30 children, were taken as hostages to the Gaza Strip with the stated goal of exchanging them for Palestinian prisoners. Many cases of rape and sexual assault were reported but Hamas denied their involvement.

Hamas said the attack was a response to
1. the continued occupation of Palestinian territories
2. the blockage of the Gaza Strip
3. the expansion of illegal Israeli settlements
4. Rising Israeli settler violence against Palestinians.

The Israelis had occupied the Gaza Strip, amongst other Palestinian territories, since the Six-Day War in 1967. Hamas, a Palestinian Islamist movement formed in 1987, is uncompromising in its stance for the complete liberation of Palestine; some scholars believe their goal to be the return of borders to 1967, others that Hamas seeks the destruction of Israel in its entirety. Saudi, Egyptian and Palestinians had warned Israel before the attack that an 'explosion' might be expected unless some political progress was made in furthering Palestinian rights and answering their claims. On 29 September Qatar, the UN and Egypt mediated an agreement to reopen crossing points to de-escalate tension. Some 17 thousand Gazans had work permits in Israel. It became clear that Hamas had plans for a much more extensive and longer occupation of Israel than eventuated.

As with the invasion by Russia of Ukraine, while Hamas outlined legitimate grievances concerning occupied land -the 4 points outlined above are legitimate concerns- there are evident weaknesses in seeking to justify the invasion, the killings and the kidnappings as complying with either the customary requirements of ius ad bellum or the various Conventions relating to commencement of war or indeed relating to its conduct, ius de bello.

What of the Israeli response? Firstly, although the argument does not appear to have been invoked by the Israelis, the right of hot dispute against belligerents in common law was confined to maritime escapades and, given the lapse of time between the raid and the Israeli response in identifying the belligerents and the kidnapped hostages, the doctrine would likely prove of limited effect. What was the nature and extent of the Israeli military response? After the Hamas raid, Israel began the bombing of the Gaza Strip. The Israeli campaign, Operation Swords of Iron, had two goals; to destroy Hamas and to liberate the hostages. More than 35 thousand Palestinians have been killed since the commencement of this Operation, with a further 10 thousand missing presumed dead. 7,800 children and 4,900 women were included in the dead. 29 thousand munitions have been dropped on Gaza, 70% of homes destroyed as well as hundreds of landmarks and numerous cemeteries. Moreover, a severe humanitarian crisis has developed; health care is in collapse, severe shortages of food and water leading to starvation, a lack of medicines, fuel and electricity. In Gaza, it is reported, there is 'no safe place'. Israel struck in places it identified as safe for the population to which to evacuate. Admittedly Hamas had an underground network, known as the metro, which housed hostages as well as combatants but was the Israelis bombardment of these and other places, above and below ground justifiable and proportionate? Indeed, the killing of 35,000 mostly civilians gave rise to accusations of Genocide under the 1948 Convention lodged with the ICJ by South Africa in May 2023 with a view, inter alia, of achieving an immediate ceasefire. That did not eventuate, but the court ordered, in its decision of January 2024, some provisional measures, without a determination of the issues of genocide but after determining that it had prima facie jurisdiction. These measures as follows, are legally binding on Israel, without appeal, although jurisdiction is now disputed:

1. Israel must take all measures within its powers to prevent acts against the convention.
2. Likewise, its military forces must comply.
3. It must prevent public incitement to genocide.
4. It must provide humanitarian relief.
5. It must prevent the destruction of any evidence relating to the Convention.
6. It must submit a report detailing action taken to comply.

While Israel's objective to eliminate Hamas appears unequivocal, it does not equate with an intention to destroy the inhabitants of Gaza. Accordingly, evidence to that effect will have to be presented to the ICJ in due course. The ICJ has no powers to enforce its judgments including the provisional measures described above.

Without doubt the raid by Hamas into Israel and the kidnapping of prisoners together with the killing of over 800 civilians was a breach of the Hague Conventions both in respect of the initiation and the atrocities inflicted thereafter.

Similarly, the killing of over 35 thousand Palestinians, the extensive destruction of homes, hospitals and heritage sites, the failure to allow humanitarian aid safe and timeous transit and the potentiality of deliberate use of starvation as a weapon of war, all constitute crimes in terms of two or more of the conventions described above.

The designation of Palestine as a state is in some doubt in international law. It is de facto recognised by a number of other states which have established bi-lateral diplomatic relations. It has been a non-member observer state at the UN since November 2012 with the General Assembly reasserting the PLO as the representative of the Palestinian people. In 2005, the Israeli Government had decided to dismantle all Israeli settlements in the Gaza Strip, a decision endorsed by the Israeli Supreme Court, holding that these settlements had been in a 'belligerent Territory'. However, the UN Human Rights Council and the Human Rights Watch reject Israel's contention that the Gaza Strip is no longer in occupation as Israel controls the airspace, waters and borders. The ICC has published a summary of evidence relating to Palestinian statehood but has itself yet to determine its own stance on the question of statehood.

What of the status of Hamas? Hamas has been in control of the Gaza Strip since 2007 and its support since the October Raid, backed by Iran, has increased and remains high. However, it has been designated a terrorist organisation by a number of states, the US in 1997, the EU in 2003.

It may be that international pressure, and no doubt the intermediacy of Qatar and Egypt, will lead to a ceasefire between Israel and Gaza with release of those remaining hostages that have survived in return for a substantial number of Palestinian prisoners held by Israel being released but it is most unlikely that the underlying conflict will be resolved or the perpetrators of killing, violence, kidnapping and torture will be brought to account. It is also evident that the destruction of so much of Gaza in addition to the killing of civilians is not proportionate nor justifiable and the need to protect the innocent was largely ignored. However, despite the prima facie criminality of actions by both sides bringing them to justice is improbable, for the reasons described.

With those powers which attempt mediation in the Israeli-Palestinian conflict, namely Qatar and Egypt in particular, there is a realisation that the return of hostages and a halt to warfare and killing and material destruction while clearly desirable and necessary, will not solve the longer-term dispute regarding the genuine grievances outlined by Hamas. But Hamas will either have to abandon its notion that Israel should not exist or be replace by a governance which does so. The recent extension of hostilities between Israel and Hezbollah in Lebanon with resultant deaths and evacuations adds a further concern to effecting peaceful and fair resolution.

It may seem appropriate for an independent commission to be established which would be charged with a responsibility of determining the facts relating to the disputes within a reasonable period and after consultation with relevant parties, and then recommending a resolution, including the establishment of a Palestinian state, the return of illegally taken lands and the payment of compensation both for land previously held by other than the current legal occupants and the for the rebuilding of Gaza infrastructure destroyed by the Israeli invasion. Ultimately these findings would be reflected in a peace treaty between the warring parties.

The UK election results in July 2024 illustrated the depth of feeling about the treatment of Gaza and the sense of frustration at the Labour Party's stance; its ambiguity in belatedly condemning this disproportionate Israeli response to the atrocities committed by Hamas. There are also misgivings about the continued sale of armaments from both the UK and USA to Israel which has failed to respond to entreaties for both a ceasefire and the conveyance of humanitarian aid.

Moreover, unless the underlying hostility to the status of both Israel and Palestine is resolved, the likelihood of further killing and civilian deaths will surely resume. Hamas, as an Islamist militant group, and Israel as, if not a theocracy, captive in the Netanyahu government, to a faction of extreme right-wing fundamentalists, are not likely to arrange a rational and lasting compromise. In addition, the conflict with Libya with Hezbollah avenging Israel's killing of their leader leading to further 'exchanges' of rockets and drones intensifies conflict in the area and raises further issues of 'just war' relating to invasion.

Turning to the Russo-Ukraine war, perhaps the ideal peace resulting in the Russian withdrawal of all troops from Ukraine and the payment of compensation for wrongful invasion, loss of innocent lives, destruction of buildings and the environment is unrealistic to envisage.

But it may be that Ukraine, for the prospect of peace and future security would be prepared to settle for less. Whether the invasion of Kursk Oblast across the

Russian Border is within the bounds of legitimate defence raises further issues for debate.

But a negotiated peace might provide for a trust territory to be established for the Don-bas with a UN force charged not only with keeping the peace but also with assessing loss and compensation and establishing an elected 'regional government'. This would provide for a referendum enabling all denizens to vote for continued membership of an independent Ukraine or associate status with Russia. Both Russia and Ukraine would be required to provide undertakings and guarantees in respect of security of borders and peace. Ukraine's future membership of NATO, or otherwise, might be part of a negotiated settlement.

Obviously, any negotiated settlement and peace treaty is fraught with difficulties, not least stemming from the lack of trust between the parties and in particular the lack of honesty of intention in respect of Russia, the hyper missile attack on a children's hospital in Kyiv being but one more recent example. Consequently, it may be that any negotiated peace may have to await a change of Government in Russia, an unlikely prospect in the short term, or a significant change of attitude and approach by the present government.

It is the Humanist position that religion, if not the opiate of the people, is sometimes the stimulus for irrational hostility to 'the other' which precludes objectivity, dialogue, empathy and compromise; all these are necessary ingredients to a lasting and constructive peace. But, however desirable, it now seems that justice and war are unlikely bedfellows.

References

Adam Shatz, Israel's Descent, London Review of Books, Vol 42, No12, 2024

Wikipedia online, 2024

Encyclopaedia Britannica online, 2024

Ziyad Hayatli, Philosophy of War in Philosophy Now, issue 124 Feb/March 2018

Brian Orend, A Just-war critique of Realism and Pacifism, Journal of Philosophical Research 26:435-477 (2001)

Hugo Grotius, On the law of War and Peace, (de Iure Belli ac Pacis), 1625; and see Wikipedia entries under Grotius and War and Peace.

Mufti Kadyroy, Press release 2022; see also Wikipedia entries, 2024.

OHCHR the Office of the High Commission for Human Rights (2024) reported in Wikipedia.

UNHCR, the United Nations High Commission for Refugees (2024)
Antonio Cassese, The 'Freedom Fighter's Problem' (in his *International Criminal Law*, 2013, 3rd ed., especially Ch. 8 on terrorism

God Riddance; A Conclusion

To many of us the world today may appear a dangerous and fearful place. The perils of war, of famine, of loss of family, of homelessness and even helplessness may appear to be increasing. While rationality, in terms of Pinker's (2018) analysis perhaps, may draw a friendlier picture, nonetheless emotionally we are responding to a narrative made more immediate by the internet, by our mobile phones, by YouTube as well as podcasts and newspapers and the myriad mechanisms for saturating our consciousness with a multitude of insecurities and unsolvable concerns.

This short book has sought to explore some of these concerns, a just war and its aftermath, a moral code and living a meaningful life, the lessons from the Stoics in addressing only those matters we are able to influence, the value of a social contract, the perils of hate speech, our obligation to sentient and other animals as part of our living environment and living without a belief in god or an afterlife.

Perhaps the prospect of an almighty guiding our thoughts and actions may bring a sense of purpose to an apparently hostile world; the bombs, the flooding, the droughts, the killings, the destruction of buildings and the environment and man's inhumanity to man may all seem part and parcel of an inconceivable and unknowable plan, beyond our reach and comprehension. But, objectively, of what consolation would this prove? Would we find solace in a vengeful god, apparently 'hell-bent' on our own destruction?

But the evidence we are now able to assemble suggests we would be unwise to trust in the concept of a God or Gods, any more than miracles or even ghouls and ghosts, search as we may. Even on a cosmic level, there is little to suggest in any purpose, any teleological plan or comprehensible meaning in its existence or beginning or end, should either be likely (see for example Tallis (2024).

Consequently, we are left with the responsibility both individually and collectively of adopting a rational approach to the issues that face us. Such does not leave us without emotional outlets; music, art, architecture, crafts as well as sport and even mountaineering, running, cycling and walking to enjoy the awe-inspiring scenery, particularly enabled by our Scottish environment. These pursuits provide a weighty counterbalancing solace to unfathomable religious doctrine and beliefs.

Moreover, the Humanist in his or her acknowledgement of a person's inter-dependence with social networks and activities seeks a path with mutual support through adversity with the challenge of self, social and environmental improvement and, as importantly through moments of joy and pleasure.
Think, absorb, contemplate, reflect, plan, engage and most earnestly enjoy!

p.s. Should you come across God in your travels, do say Hello; and wish him, her, it or they all the best; they need it, and their track record suggests they will also need a lot of outside help. The humanist and others may seek to provide this on earth; otherwise, in the cosmic control room, God is alone!

Pinker, Steven, Enlightenment Now, Penguin Books, 2019
Tullis, Raymond, Does the Cosmos Have a Purpose? Philosophy Now, Issue 162, June/July, 2024.

INDEX

A

Animal Welfare, 4, 63, 68, 72
Atheism, 15, 16

C

Climate Change, 74, 83, 84, 90, 91, 92

D

Democracy, 61

E

Education, 6
Equality, 39
Ethics, 7, 70, 73

F

Freedom, 26, 33, 34, 56, 67, 103, 109, 122

G

God, 1, 2, 3, 4, 6, 7, 17, 18, 35, 46, 60, 61, 94, 95, 107, 123, 124

H

Hate Crime, 4
Human Rights, 11, 12, 13, 26, 32, 33, 34, 35, 39, 114, 115, 119, 121
Humanism, 4, 5, 6, 7, 8, 9, 10, 11, 12, 13, 14, 15, 16, 93

I

Independence, 4, 36, 47, 48

J

Just War, 4, 105, 106, 107
Justice, 24, 53, 56, 58, 59, 61, 62, 73, 79, 114

M

Matter, 4, 16, 35, 73, 97
Mind, 4, 98, 100, 102, 103
Morality, 10, 18, 22

N

Nationalism, 4, 36, 47, 48

P

Philosophy, 5, 7, 16, 21, 22, 62, 72, 73, 97, 104, 121, 124

R

Reason, 58, 95
Reform, 47, 49, 83
Religion, 33, 52
Rights, 26, 27, 31, 32, 33, 35, 39, 47, 63, 67, 69, 72, 73, 114, 115, 119

S

Science, 9, 73
Secularism, 11
Social Contract, 4, 49, 52, 53, 56
Society, 1, 2, 3, 24, 34, 35
Stoicism, 93, 94, 95, 96, 97